Build-A-BAE-R (Bae Edition)

Stuffed Hearts & Hollow Love

Monique R. Darnell

Edited by
Nicole Queen

VISION PUBLISHING
HOUSE

Vision Publishing House
support@vision-publishinghouse.com
www.vision-publishinghouse.com

ISBN: 978-1-955297-97-4 (print)
LCCN: 2025917097

*I dedicate this book to the woman
who no longer builds for love,
but becomes it...*

I am no longer accepting the things I cannot change. I am changing the things I cannot accept.

— Angela Davis

Contents

Heart-to-Heart

A Letter From One Sister to Another

Dear Beloved Reader,

I hope this book serves as a guide through any abandonment, rejection, or emotional neglect you may have faced. My aim is for it to help you reclaim your self-worth and build healthy, fulfilling relationships from the inside out. Read this book and find hope—there is a way forward. You don't have to settle, and you still have time. You are worthy of love right now, and you don't need to create a perfect partner to receive it. Channel the energy you've directed toward others into building yourself. Be everything you've ever wanted, and remember that you are already THAT GIRL!

Love,
Your sister, Monique

Introduction
Before You Build

If you picked up this book, chances are you're Barbara the Builder, working at the nearest Build-A-BAE-R shop in town. Haha, yup! That was me! No tea, no shade… we've all been there. Some are still there now, which is why I wrote this book. This isn't a guide to getting a man or building your own; it's about helping you see yourself clearly. The truth is, many of us build relationships from broken pieces—relationships based on conditional manipulation, relationships formed from bloody hands, where we sacrifice parts of ourselves to build him, calling it "ride or die" when it's dysfunction and trauma bonding. But not today, sis. Not after this book!

I wrote this book because I was that girl—the PICK ME, CHOOSE ME, LOVE ME girl—and I didn't even realize it. I appeared successful on paper, but deep down, I was the one trying to be lovable enough to make someone stay. I tried to be attractive enough for him to choose me and remain. I did everything a wife would do to prove I was worthy of his commitment. I remember what it was like to abandon yourself while trying to prove you're worth loving. It wasn't that long ago that I transformed into this woman. So, I thought I'd share what I learned, what I experienced, and how to escape, as well as track the growth from today's life lessons.

This book was birthed from my fears and my abandonment stories. Build-A-BAE-R (Bae Edition) is not a rulebook for dating; rather, it aims to shift the world's perspectives on trauma and how it affects who we date, what we do, how we love, and how we show up in the world. This book seeks to raise awareness and create a safe space for self-reflection and evaluation—a pause in action to choose yourself over your past. It's about living a life of abundance rather than scarcity or thinking, "whoever is going to love me is going to love me." It's a call to be brave and to stop allowing fear to dictate your life. It's a movement—to position yourself to experience the love that was created in the beginning: a love without conditions. A love where all your flaws, quirks, and even your insecurities can still be embraced. So that you can be free to be whoever you are, from safe and soft to thoughtful and adored. Whether sourced from within or from others, it's yours. You don't have to earn it or work for it—it was given freely from the start.

It is now 2025, and I am gathering all the fragments, all the mirror conversations, the moments when I dragged myself out, crying and fearful, because I am choosing me. I am changing my perspective, embracing my role as a trailblazer, and accepting my calling. I had to learn how to nurture myself, support myself, find my voice, and advocate for my needs. I had to protect Monique, show up for myself, recognize my worth, and understand that I don't have to settle. I needed to reparent the little girl who was waiting to be picked up off the floor and reclaim the woman I was always meant to be. The woman I am today. The woman who is writing to you.

The woman… We are. I am. You are… the Woman!

This is a call to action. No longer Barbra the Builder. No more overcompensating to make things work. No more equating productivity with love. No more accepting the bare minimum while still not having that minimum met. No more chaos. No more self-sabotage to prove that they love you because they stayed or because of "chemistry." It's for the woman who dares to say, "I don't have to hold you down or fix him," but instead chooses to believe in and walk in her own truths.

So, if you're reading this and your heart is tired and you want to give up but hope won't let you, I say—I was you. You don't have to beg for love. You don't have to build another man from broken pieces because you've been conditioned to accept less and be humble. You don't have to settle for whatever comes your way just because the alternative is shame or embarrassment about a failed relationship, being 40 and unmarried, or being a single mother alone with your dog or cat. You get to be whole. You get to choose yourself. And you get to wait for love that sees all of you and doesn't flinch.

Let's rebuild from wholeness, not wounds.

Before we embark on this journey together, let me share this with you and let it resonate in your heart: to the parts of you that are still hurting, still questioning, still hoping, and still healing—you don't have to be whole and healed to want better. You can start now. Right now! You don't have to shrink to be chosen. You don't have to change into someone else with each new partner to be more lovable. You don't have to be quieter, more chill, more submissive, or more willing to give your body just to keep a man who isn't even ready.

Understand this, my beautiful, loving, and caring sister—you were never created to fix broken men at the expense of breaking yourself. You are worthy and deserving of love in its truest form— soft, safe, and seen. But first, sis… you've got to choose you. Not the survival version. Not the abandoned version. Not the hot girl summer version. But you… all of you. Not the masked-up, hyper-independent version. You.

This is the journey we are on, and I'm walking it with you.

Part One

The Workshop

Station 1

Welcome to Build-A-BAE-R
Where My Building Workshop Began

I n this chapter, I invite you into the raw beginnings of my realization that what I thought was strength was often self-protection dressed up in "I'm good" energy. You'll walk with me through the first time I felt the sting of abandonment without knowing its name. The fear. The disorientation. The compulsion to move on quickly rather than sit with the ache. This isn't just about a breakup; it's about the moment I began to recognize the deeper blueprint of my emotional pain, and the survival patterns I'd built my love life around.

This station sets the foundation for everything that follows. We can't heal what we won't name. So together, let's trace the roots of the workshop, the heartbreak, the confusion, the armor and begin the sacred task of returning to ourselves.

* * *

The first time I realized I was suffering from abandonment wounds, I didn't fully understand what it was. All I felt was fear. I was afraid of the physical sensation, which I now recognize as breakup anxiety. Back then, abandonment felt like an empty pit in my soul. I couldn't focus on anything but the pain and fear of being left. The confusion of being abandoned overwhelmed me, and at that time, I didn't grasp its effects; I was merely in survival mode. My mindset was "On to the next" and "Oh well."

The abandonment cut deep because I was raised in an environment where I felt "fat, Black, and bald-headed." I grew up as the daughter who was treated like the black sheep, which kept me on guard and in survival mode. It hindered my ability to believe in and receive love.

In 2021, I learned that experiences from my childhood could be the root of my fears of abandonment. At that time, I had a best friend named Key-Key. We were very close and talked every day—literally every day and every moment we could. Being therapists ourselves only fueled our conversations, allowing us to explore how to handle various situations! One day, responding from my abandonment wounds while in therapist mode, I was processing my thoughts. Key-Key said to me, "Girl, you really ought to write a book about abandonment because you are an expert on that."

I never realized abandonment could manifest in this way, and I thought it would be a valuable teaching moment for anyone who might be experiencing it. Initially, I brushed off her suggestion, but then the therapist in me began to process it—asking myself questions, wondering why I was acting the way I was, and trying to understand why my words didn't align with my body language. This prompted me to sit down and reflect: when and where did these feelings originate? It wasn't until I attended a training course for my certifications that I came across some enlightening information. So, back to the events of my childhood—yeah.

When I was young, we didn't have much, and that felt normal. We lived in a little blue house near the church, surrounded by beautiful but bothersome flowers. The flowers attracted numerous big bumblebees, which was quite annoying. We didn't have much, and that was okay; after all, how could a child aged four to six under-stand what poverty truly looked like? We didn't even have a dining room table, so the kids sat on the floor on newspapers, separated from the adults, sometimes even in different rooms.

My brothers devoured their food like garbage cans while I, the only girl, often found myself alone on the floor because, back then, you couldn't express your likes or dislikes—and I didn't eat eggs. In my mother's house, wasting food was not an option, so I frequently sat in that dark room, unable to voice my feelings. In a Black Southern household, you had no rights; you did as you were told, or a whipping awaited. Many nights and days, I remained there on the floor, forced to swallow food I didn't want so I could finally get up and leave.

I cried, but no one heard me. No one cared.

This marked the beginning of my pain and my complicated relationship with abandonment. I learned that no one would or could save me; if you didn't do what others wanted, you would be left alone—in a room, crying and afraid. I experienced darkness both physically and emotionally. I also realized that boys received special treatment since my brothers were allowed outside. At the time, I didn't understand that they got to go out because they finished their food. All I saw was how I wasn't allowed to join them and how I was the one being scolded—alone.

And that was the beginning of the A-BAN-DO-MENT! Yes, that much emphasis. Why, you ask? Because since that day, I have been fighting for my life—fighting to be seen, fighting to be valued. You see, because I didn't like eggs, I refused to eat them. As a result, I was left alone in a room, forced to eat them, with no option to leave until I did.

At this moment, while sitting on the side of my bed, facing the window, I am battling fear—fear of exhaustion. "Let's stop right now." I cry because I don't want to confront this—fear of judgment, fear of isolation. Every day, I must do the work; every day, I fight to keep abandonment at bay. I believed there was more—something beyond this. A voice kept whispering, "There has to be more. This can't be it." This relentless search for change kept me trapped in a cycle of pain for years—until I finally sat down to examine myself and my actions, initiating the journey toward change.

Writing this book, I now realize that my abandonment wounds didn't originate with me—they are inherited trauma, pain, and disappointment connected to experiences that I now use as strength to help others. This awareness comes from hard work, healing, maintaining an open mind for growth, and refusing to settle.

Now that I'm here, I can see that little Monique learned—whether directly or indirectly—that in the little blue house, boys received whatever they wanted. They were treated better. I felt alone, an unwanted, dark-skinned little girl. In middle school, I discovered that I was only valued for my body. Poverty was tied to my living situation, the lack of material possessions, my family background, and my unkempt hair. I was alone in middle school, learning that I was unwanted, which triggered a cycle of people-pleasing—begging, doing anything to avoid loneliness. In some childhood situations, I was left to fend for myself; even as an adult, the message was clear: "Figure it out," a phrase often uttered by my mother. This left me feeling emotionally and physically isolated.

As I grew older, I unknowingly made a vow to myself that I would never feel that pain again—the ache, the stillness in time, the fear and darkness that haunted me repeatedly. I became the girl who would do whatever it took to survive. This meant learning how to shapeshift, to be whatever others needed me to be so they wouldn't leave. I wanted to "stunt on them hoes" (my favorite line) and be low-maintenance, not asking for anything.

Growing up in the South, being dark-skinned was an additional challenge. At the time, my hair was long and luscious, but as I got older, it began to break and become damaged. This fueled my insecurities and thoughts of hiding—not making myself known. I had to be the girl who was always available, quickly learning that any attention—whether harmful or positive—was still attention, so I stayed out of the way. I learned to equate touch with love and affection, confusing availability and access with importance, believing that importance meant they wouldn't leave.

When attention, affection, and love walked out (as they often did), I lost a piece of myself. I caved in, crucifying myself with agony, pain, and resurfacing fears of unexplained, unidentified, and uncommunicated expectations, realities, and conditioned truths. I thought that if I just had a hotter body, if I could give more, or if I earned this degree, they would need me and not abandon me. I believed that if I just gave and did more, maybe they'd stay.

As I continued to grow, I told myself it had to get better. Don't give up. Keep trying. I didn't realize I was building my relationships on a foundation of abandonment. I kept choosing partners who mirrored the very fear I was trying to escape or prove something to. They were emotionally unavailable, inconsistent, or simply took what was available. I dismissed it with an "Oh well, I'll just find another one."

I thought if I could fix them and help them with their needs—essentially being a helpmate—they would stay. But the truth was, I was choosing men who were beneath my aspirations, who couldn't satisfy my goals and ambition. I was settling for whoever wanted me. In fact, I completely gave up on the idea of love, convincing myself that meeting certain criteria was enough.

At the time, I didn't realize that I wasn't dating to be loved—I was dating to be right. I wanted to prove that nothing was wrong with me and that I was better than all the people who bullied or rejected me. I thought, "I'll show them." This mindset created years of "stunting on them hoes" and constant relationships, but I never truly learned or understood that I was dating to be saved, to be seen and valued, and to be rescued from that dining room floor, crying and forced to eat eggs alone in the dark.

I wanted a hero—someone to stand up for me when I couldn't stand up for myself. I wanted someone to stay when I didn't even know how to stay with myself.

It wasn't until my daughter started getting older, allowing me to focus on what was happening in my life and work on coming out of survival mode, that I could finally see what my mom had always been saying to me. She would tell me, "YOU'RE THE PROB-LEM." But because I felt hurt, abandoned, and kicked out at 18—once again not being chosen—I wasn't able to see it. I was angry and upset that all I ever wanted was love: someone to adore me, to work things out with me, and to stick it out with me no matter what —even if I didn't want the eggs.

Eventually, I was able to grasp the truth behind what my mother was saying. Yes, she could have conveyed it in a more loving and supportive way, but it is what it is. You can't make people be who you want them to be. You either see them for who they are and accept that—acceptance doesn't mean approval; it just means you stop going back and forth with what is—or you miss out on having a mom.

So, I chose to hear what she was saying and work on my perspective. That's when it hit me. What if I heard my mom from a loving and nurturing standpoint? What if I stopped seeing her as someone trying to hurt me and let my guard down? What if how I received things was within my power?

I shifted my perspective to receive love and began to question, "How could I be the problem?" As this thought flowed through my body, I realized that my feelings of being unwanted and unworthy were the reasons I chose the men I did. These feelings stemmed from unhealed abandonment wounds from my childhood.

A lot changed when my daughter turned 18. I felt freed to focus on myself; she was no longer my sole identity or focal point. As a single parent, my primary responsibility had been to care for her. She was my life, and I needed to protect her, which also gave me something to love and receive love in return. However, subconsciously, due to my upbringing and unhealed experiences, I had become a single parent myself, shaped by a survival-mode mindset and the lessons I learned growing up.

It wasn't until 2020, when everyone was forced to slow down and Camille was around 15 or 16, that I realized my life was miserable because of my own choices. During a conversation meant to console my daughter, I recognized that my own thoughts about myself kept me trapped in this misery. I constantly battled the core belief of "Who's going to love me?" I feared rejection and abandonment, and I believed that people only treat you the way you treat yourself. I found myself pleading with others to love me out of this fear, unaware of the wounds I carried.

Not long after I had my daughter, I contracted HSV-2, genital herpes, which became a significant part of my identity. I felt abandoned again and questioned, "Who's going to love me now?" This added another layer of brokenness, low self-esteem, and the belief that I would have to work for love and settle for less because who would want me now? It diminished any sense of worth I thought I had. I felt alone—again. And unwanted—again.

It took some time, but after I wrote my first book, From Fact to Faith, in 2019, my journey of self-acceptance related to my diagnosis truly began. I realized that I was showing up scared and with low self-esteem, and I put myself out there in that state—and people treated me accordingly. Later, I learned that I also attracted that treatment. Oh God—the tears, the realization, and the empathy I developed for myself.

During this time, I became increasingly aware of abandonment, which later became something I could rely on—a friend that never left. Often, I found myself choosing people I knew would confirm my feelings of abandonment, just to validate my beliefs and keep myself trapped in a cycle of self-harm, extinguishing any hope for something better.

Thus, the journey of grappling with abandonment continued, but I remained unaware. This lack of awareness hindered any chance for change, perpetuating the cycle of loneliness I struggled so hard to overcome, along with the feelings of not being wanted.

Station 2

Name Your Bae

Uncovering the Root of What (and Who) You're Attracted To

Attraction isn't always about love it's often about familiarity. This station helps you pause and reflect: Why am I drawn to this? The answer is rarely just about charm or chemistry. It's about history yours.

When abandonment becomes your norm, you start calling inconsistency passion, and chaos excitement. "Naming your bae" means identifying not just the person, but the pattern they represent. It's about noticing when your heart feels drawn to what feels familiar even when it hurts.

This is where awareness begins. Not to shame yourself, but to free yourself.

*   *   *

Abandonment is not merely the act of someone physically leaving you; it runs much deeper. It's when someone looks you in the eyes and says, "I got you," only to ghost you the next day. It's going to school, believing you have a friend who has your back, only to discover by the end of the day that they've teamed up with someone else to talk about you. It's being left home alone at a young age for hours, worrying and relying on the little you know about surviving because your mother has to work long hours without the funds for a sitter or enough family support to help.

It's the small things that cut deep—the conversations that never happened: the "How are you?" the "Where are you?" the "What can I do for you?" It's about being denied emotional security by someone who didn't even realize the impact of their actions, leaving you to question your worth and your capacity for love. It's the father who was physically present but mentally and emotionally absent. It's the father who wasn't there at all, and the mother who covered for him, leading you to develop a distorted understanding of what love truly is. It's the church that welcomed your tithes and gifts but over-looked your tears.

Abandonment manifests as the absence of genuine action—intimacy disguised by the performance of care, a hollow echo of love wrapped in false pretenses. It's when presence fails to match connection, creating an illusion of intimacy. It's silence masquerading as love.

As a Black woman, this experience is often concealed beneath expectations and generational duties to care, give, and do. We are seen but not valued, clothed but not comforted, loved out of obligation but never fully embraced. You learn that the norm is to have insufficient support, and you become accustomed to it. You lean into it and adapt—because what other choice is there?

You learn that not being chosen does not reflect your worth. Being emotionally unfriended while still physically present is a reality of life—and it's a normal experience for a little Black girl. By the time a child is 8 years old, they have already begun to form an understanding of the world: how to navigate it, what feels safe, and what they must do to avoid upsetting their parents.

This knowledge is shaped by their environment, upbringing, and the interplay of nature and nurture—the things they absorb, feel, and internalize from the unspoken messages in their homes, schools, churches, and communities. The unspoken lessons we learn become integral to our makeup, shaping our perspectives, lenses, and core beliefs. They are birthed and nurtured in the subconscious, ultimately forming a person's characteristics, identity, and worldview—defining their core values and beliefs. This process influences how a child perceives themselves and how they expect others to treat them.

In middle school, children begin to develop a deeper awareness of themselves and those around them. They are easily influenced by the subconscious lessons they have internalized. At this age, they may not recognize that their experiences—what they see, feel, and hear—are being stored in their mental vault of reality. This vault operates discreetly, accumulating lessons that are meant to keep them safe, though they may struggle to articulate these feelings.

I believe we are at a time when people are more emotionally attuned and educated, leading to increased conscientiousness about their words and actions. They understand that their behavior can impact others, whether intentionally or unintentionally. A child left alone in a dark space, feeling unseen and unheard, may express, "I feel unwanted." This feeling, often unrecognized, can manifest in ways that affect them later in life—such as shrinking themselves, people-pleasing, or misinterpreting gestures, behaviors, and words as expressions of love.

These experiences become embedded in a child's subconscious as guidelines for what to do or avoid—ways to receive love or to feel unloved. A child who is praised for their actions may come to believe, "The more I do, the more I am seen, and the more I am loved." This belief establishes the core idea that productivity equals love, leading to behaviors such as codependency, fear of abandonment, and fear of rejection.

The root of these beliefs lies in childhood and how love was perceived. The lessons learned during this time are deeply ingrained in the subconscious. This can also lead to behaviors aimed at understanding and interpreting others' actions due to the silent lessons learned from past experiences.

During this formative period, the brain is functioning as expected—learning, becoming more aware, developing social skills, and forming connections. However, in the background, the subconscious continues to communicate without words.

While the conscious mind may express a desire for friendship, saying, "I want friends; let's be friendly," the subconscious often shuts that desire down due to learned behaviors of rejection and abandonment. As a result, the child may withdraw and isolate themselves when they truly wish to express themselves and connect with others.

By this stage, the child has internalized several beliefs:

- To be loved, I must be perfect.
- To feel safe, I must remain unseen.
- To avoid being talked about, I must talk about others.
- To be loved, I must allow physical touch.

When children navigate these experiences, they may blame themselves or internalize their feelings due to their inability to self-regulate, contextualize, or process rejection and abandonment.

At this age, children learn about love, compassion, and the concepts of good and bad, right and wrong, ugly and beautiful. These lessons stem from their upbringing. If a child does not receive secure love and attachment, they may grow up facing attachment and relationship issues.

My role is not to assign blame but to raise awareness so that you can break the cycle and learn to address the gaps, voids, and needs in your life, rather than allowing feelings of abandonment to become your comfort.

Experiencing repeated rejection for various reasons can distort your self-confidence and self-perception, affecting your sense of worth. This creates an internal emptiness that you may attempt to fill with people, places, or things.

As stated before, what you learned in childhood and how you were loved created a narrative embedded in your subconscious that shapes your perspective and perception—ultimately becoming your reality. You begin to understand love by practicing what you observe in your environment, which also defines what feels safe. The basic needs you learned in childhood—how to endure without—develop because, at that age, you're not mature enough to comprehend what's truly happening.

In fact, the reason I'm writing this book is that there isn't enough awareness regarding behaviors, childhood experiences, and the factors that influence how we choose our partners.

Women are often viewed as emotional beings, and I do not deny that. However, some are ruled by empathy, and I am one of them. I learned at a young age that I was overly sensitive, but I didn't fully accept or understand it until much later.

I later discovered that empathy without boundaries is self-destructive. I also learned that while my emotions are real, they are not always true.

For a long time, my emotions dictated my actions and led me to dark places, reinforcing the beliefs I held about myself—that no one loved me and no one wanted me.

But today—just now—I had an epiphany. As I navigate my current experiences, I realize that writing this book is not only for you but also for me!

This is healing. (In Christian terms: it is delivering me.)

I was talking to myself—engaging with the many parts of my being: my mind, my will, my emotions, and my physical self. As I processed my thoughts and behaviors, I noticed something significant. The things I was writing in this book prompted reflection. I told my emotions: You can't drive the bus anymore. You may have driven the Mercedes, but in this next chapter, you can't drive the Range Rover.

Then, it clicked. Could my emotions be what my subconscious is feeding me? Is it still my subconscious that is driving the bus? Are my emotions merely a response to and reflection of my core beliefs, my narrative—things learned in childhood that are now embedded in my subconscious?

Am I longing for something that was never healed in my subconscious?

Healing the abandonment wound goes deeper than merely working on self-esteem or self-worth. It involves choosing myself instead of clinging to false security in a relationship—or anything else I have absorbed from my subconscious.

It's about breaking the lie in my narrative that I must be married to be somebody.

It's recognizing that the clouds still move in the sky and the world continues to spin. All of this happens without me needing to prove, give, sacrifice, or beg.

Does anyone want to buy a heart? (K. Michelle album reference)

It's about maturing—sitting with myself and choosing the hurt and pain that stand up for me, rather than opting for the pain that ignores my suffering and fighting for others to prove my worth.

Healing abandonment wounds and reclaiming yourself involves understanding the subconscious.

It requires recognizing what you lost to cope with the pain and what you used to fill the void.

The unspoken beliefs and narratives that were instilled in you still influence how you choose your partner.

Somewhere along the way, you learned to believe that this was all you could have.

In fact, you were taught, "This is a good man, Savannah," leading you to lower your standards. You were encouraged to appreciate what you have because there aren't enough Black men to go around. While this emphasizes the experiences of Black women and culture, I believe the underlying message taught women to settle and be grateful, ultimately conditioning us to submit and obey in ways that stifled our hopes, dreams, and aspirations.

This has created a wave of women accepting little to nothing—just breadcrumbs. We sympathize with men to receive whatever they can give, because we are nurturers who can make something out of nothing.

But this is only true for unhealed and hurt women.

When you finish this book, my hope is that you identify where the seed—or event—was planted and uproot it. I aim to provide a safe space for you to be vulnerable and transparent, to become aware, and to ask questions of all parts of yourself: mentally, emotionally, physically, spiritually (including religion and the subconscious), and financially.

I want to help you change your perspective and perception, which in turn can change your life. Seek therapy. Heal your wounds. Envision, create, and build a new identity. Rebrand and practice this new identity. Embrace freedom, life, and love in ways you never knew existed.

Abandonment manifests in your thoughts when you check your phone and find no messages. It thrives in the silence—and the noise—of fear. It is buried beneath the duties and expectations of the day, moving through your hours without a voice, yet still aching in the presence of a whisper:

"You messed up again."

"You made a mistake."

"What did you do wrong?"

It embodies the essence of survival, drawing from learned behaviors of childhood and the validation of false narratives and core beliefs. It fosters that unspoken belief that you were forgotten, that you weren't enough, that they don't like you.

Now that we recognize it's embedded in our subconscious, what do we call this event?

I'll tell you: TRAUMA.

I believe trauma is any event or experience that alters your perspective—how you respond and engage with the world—in a negative way.

However, some traumatic events—situations and circumstances—can lead to positive change. Yet, in my view, they are still trauma. Trauma can reshape what lies in the subconscious, rewriting the narrative for better or worse. The primary objective of trauma is to teach the body how to survive.

Let's discuss the neurological aspect—the physical part. This, in my opinion, often takes the longest to change.

Remember when I mentioned five components? I believe there are five fundamental parts that make up a human being:

1. Mental
2. Emotional
3. Physical
4. Spiritual (religion/subconscious)
5. Financial

We've spent considerable time discussing the spiritual and subconscious. Now, let's take the next step and focus on the physical.

Here's how it works: the mind operates as it wishes—thinking, functioning, going about its day. The body follows suit until it says, "I don't want to do anything"—for example, feeling tired, overwhelmed, or groggy. At this point, the mind must decide: do I want to heed what the body is saying?

Next, the emotions chime in: "I don't feel like getting up. I just want to lie here."

Meanwhile, the subconscious remains largely unaffected—until it's time to make some significant changes.

Then the mind exclaims, "I'm tired of feeling this way. I make up my mind to change, yet I self-sabotage. Ugh, what's going on? I want to change, but I can't. Why can't I?"

Because the subconscious has learned something that contradicts the conscious mind, it resists changing its beliefs or makeup.

This is when the real work begins.

The body acts according to its own desires.

The emotions feel what they want.

The mind thinks what it wants.

However, until the subconscious is challenged, behavior won't change.

The body remembers what happened, and the subconscious reinforces those memories, causing the body to respond instinctively —without the mind even engaging.

Thus, survival mode kicks in.

It remembers how to stay safe, leading you to enter this mode without realizing it. Meanwhile, emotions accompany you on this journey, tagging the mind and expressing stress and depression—reflecting how they feel. All the while, the subconscious directs each part of you without uttering a word.

Now, let's delve deeper.

You're not dysfunctional. You're not crazy.

You simply taught yourself how to survive.

You learned how to protect yourself.

When something traumatic occurs—such as abandonment, betrayal, rejection, or emotional neglect—your brain records it. It gets embedded in the vault, never to be forgotten or experienced again. However, if this contradicts a deep need, it creates a perpetual, toxic cycle.

For example: "I want love. I want to be married."

But what's embedded in your subconscious is: "Whenever someone falls in love, they get abandoned. They end up broke. They become vulnerable. They depend on someone who can leave and hurt them."

So what does the subconscious instruct the body to do?

- Don't let anyone close.
- Build walls.
- Sabotage relationships to test if they truly love you.

Let's break this down further:

1. The Amygdala: Your Alarm System

This part of your brain sets off the alarm, alerting other areas that something is wrong—you're triggered. Have you ever had a good day, only to be thrown back in time by a song or a scent? That's why you feel as if you're reliving that moment, even if it happened years ago. The alarm has sounded.

2. The Hippocampus: The Vault

Think of this as your brain's vault—filled with memories, experiences, and events. But when trauma strikes, the system becomes scrambled. The event doesn't get properly filed away; it's like a bored security guard roaming the halls, manifesting as tension in your chest and neck because it was ignored and never addressed. Now, it shows up wherever it wants.

3. The Prefrontal Cortex: Your Logic Voice (The Mind)

This is the voice that questions, "Why do I feel like this? I'm in the car, not even thinking about him. He must be thinking about me. Ugh." Or, "Why am I still bothered or worried about him? I'm not going to call—he has my number. I'm good."

This part helps you think clearly, but when trauma hits or a trigger resurfaces, this voice either quiets down or becomes irrational.

You know this person lacks the capacity to love you, yet your body reacts with fear and tension. You worry they'll leave or not choose you, leading to instability, anxiety, and anxious behaviors—all in an effort to prevent what you fear: abandonment.

So why do you keep replaying the past? Because you haven't taken the power away from the event—the trauma.

To heal from something like that, you must first acknowledge its effects.

Acknowledge it.

Give it grace.

You're not crazy.

You're not overreacting.

But you are reliving it.

It's hidden in your nervous system, triggering your fight or flight response.

I bet you didn't know that, huh? This is where the five parts come in. Healing isn't just about talking; it's not surface-level. It must address each part because trauma manifests in each of them. You have to heal and learn how to feel safe again.

Station 3

Pick the Heart

How Abandonment Wounds Shape Your Love Blueprint

In this station, we explore how your earliest wounds silently shape your love life. Unhealed abandonment doesn't just echo in your memories it shows up in your patterns, your preferences, and your "type." Without healing, you don't just fall in love you reenact.

This chapter invites you to trace how your heart learned to love: what it craved, what it feared, and what it accepted as normal. The people you choose aren't random they reflect the blueprint etched by your earliest emotional experiences. But the good news is, once you see the pattern, you can begin to rewire it.

* * *

What you didn't heal in childhood will manifest in who you date, how you love, and what you ultimately settle for. You will find yourself dating the same type of person repeatedly—it's the same picture but a different frame. This pattern becomes your lifestyle, your characteristics, your TYPE. If you don't address the root cause, you will keep watering the wrong fruit.

By this point in your life, you have realized that abandonment is not just about physical absence. It goes beyond someone leaving you or not choosing you; it has become part of your identity. It permeates every area of your life: the way you present yourself, how you perceive the world, and how you engage with it.

You are not crazy, flawed, or broken—your core beliefs and narrative are still shaped by childhood trauma. Sometimes, the lie becomes the law, leading you to believe in what has happened to you, which then forms your identity. This process teaches you to learn from your pain, creating a sense of protection that transforms into a new belief—a law.

For instance, you might think: They always leave. I am too much or too extra. I am too emotional. No one ever stays. Needing someone makes you vulnerable, and vulnerability is equated with weakness. From that pain and rejection, you consciously decide to respond based on that belief.

If your belief is that you are too much or too extra, you may hold parts of yourself back, never fully trusting or allowing yourself to experience true love or even pain. You might merely go through the motions. If someone tells you that you are "too needy," you create an unspoken law in your heart, mind, and soul that says, I will never be needy again—thus, I will never face that kind of hurt again. Even if this law causes you more pain, it remains in place until something changes.

Years may pass, and nothing shifts. Do you know why? Because it has become your identity—your story—something you live out and embody. You start to excel at this narrative, knowing when to leave. You develop thoughts like: I'll show them. Never again will someone reject me. I get to choose now, and nobody will ever abandon me again.

This narrative becomes the lens through which everything is filtered, causing issues even in healthy relationships, which ironically become the biggest threat.

Have you ever found yourself self-sabotaging something because it seemed too good to be true?

We'll explore that more in this chapter.

Let's discuss core beliefs and narratives. What are they? Core beliefs are formed assumptions and beliefs about yourself and the world. They shape how you interpret events, influencing your emotions, reactions, and decisions. These beliefs are typically established in childhood and dictate how you perceive situations—what you believe you deserve, how you give and receive love, and what you tolerate, expect, or fear.

Narratives are the stories you tell yourself to understand your life and experiences, which are generated from those beliefs. The narratives we create often influence our thoughts, emotions, and behaviors. While these beliefs may not always be vocalized, you can gauge what a person believes based on their actions.

When a child experiences abandonment, neglect, rejection, or abuse, it profoundly affects their self-perception and worldview, altering who they can become later in life. Core beliefs and narratives linger in the background, guiding the individual on how to stay safe based on the information they've internalized. These unspoken beliefs can dictate decision-making.

Now, let's review some core beliefs.

The biggest revelation I had during my healing journey occurred when I read *You Are a Badass* by Jen Sincero. I realized that my beliefs about relationships led me to low-key self-sabotage them because, deep down, I didn't truly want them. My core belief was that love was cruel and dangerous.

Why, you ask?

Because I witnessed my mom struggle with love. She has been married four times, and if you've picked up on that by now, you might think, "Oh, this could explain her challenges in relationships," and you would be right. But that's not the focus of this discussion and will be addressed later.

Given the hardships we faced due to the men in my mom's life, I learned that love equated to vulnerability, and vulnerability led to hardship, pain, homelessness, and struggle. So, whenever I entered a relationship that was genuinely good—meaning healthy—I would panic. Deep down, I feared it and what I believed it required to sustain it. I worried I would end up homeless, broke, and abandoned, just as I had seen my mom suffer.

As a single parent, my priority was to care for my daughter, which meant avoiding that fate. Consequently, I would sabotage the relationship. Ironically, I would venture back out there and do it all over again! I would date and engage with someone because I felt obligated to, not wanting to be seen as the problem or incapable of keeping a partner, all while failing to realize that nothing would change until I changed my belief system.

So, what did I do? I dug deeper, but not in a constructive way. I started internalizing the negative narrative: What's wrong with me? I'm too emotional. I'm the problem. This core belief was rooted in my experiences with my mother, pushing me to work harder to prove myself—to make someone choose me and stay with me.

I strove to make myself indispensable—becoming the savior, the hero, doing more—so that he couldn't abandon me. I connected my abandonment wound to the belief that I was hard to love, that I needed to be perfect to receive love. Then, with my HSV diagnosis, I thought: I can only get what I can get, and that must be the best I can achieve, because who is going to love me now? I had barely managed to have someone accept me before, and now I had to expose myself to potential rejection.

This affected how I communicated my diagnosis to others. Because I viewed myself this way, I presented myself this way—and they rejected me because I was pleading, asking, "Anybody wanna buy a heart?" (a reference to the K. Michelle album).

Fearing rejection, I showed up with tears and fear—and because I was scared, they felt scared too.

When I realized that I—myself—was making my life miserable due to my self-perception, I made a spoken contract with myself: I will never live another miserable day by my own hand. I refused to let my self-image dictate my happiness because people only see what I choose to present to them—and I vowed to change that.

Due to unhealed abandonment wounds, we often validate the narratives and fears within us. We gravitate toward familiar pains, reinforcing our core beliefs and narratives, which ultimately define who we are.

For instance, a woman with the belief that people always leave may cling too tightly to someone new or refuse to open up at all. A woman who believes all men are dogs may continue dating without making any changes, expecting to be treated poorly because that is what she believes men are meant to be.

From a therapeutic perspective, abandonment encompasses emotional neglect (being present but unavailable), inconsistent care or affection, unmet emotional needs, betrayal or broken trust, and feelings of being unseen, unheard, or unsupported.

You might have thought abandonment was simply about someone not choosing you or leaving, right? It can be so much more.

For example, I uncovered another layer of abandonment for myself in 2023. I was speaking with my daughter about how much her father loved her, and the conversation quickly escalated into a heated exchange. She began to cry and said, "If that is what love is, I don't want it."

She continued by saying that, because I told her all those years that her father loved her—even though he didn't reach out, didn't send anything for her birthdays, or even call—it caused her to settle in so many ways. That was her understanding of love.

It completely shook my foundation because I thought I was doing the right thing—trying to keep her from hating her father by telling her he loved her, trusting that one day she would see who he really was on her own. What I was really trying to do was avoid being the bad guy. I didn't want to speak negatively about her father to her.

Ultimately, though, it created an abandonment wound for my daughter—teaching her to accept breadcrumbs as love because her mom told her so.

The conversation then turned to me and how not having my own father was the beginning of my abandonment issues. But he died—how was that his fault? Well, studies suggest that death can be a form of abandonment.

This was something I couldn't control or change. I just accepted what my mother told me about my father: that he loved me and that I was his favorite—out of nine children at the time.

I then put my therapy hat on and started revisiting my childhood. I remembered how my dad's side of the family didn't really like or accept me. A few people did—my great-grandmother and great-grandfather—but my dad's mom was not fond of me.

My uncle and one aunt—who is my aunt on both sides of the family (weird, but not my job to figure out)—accepted me. However, the main aunt kind of just tolerated me.

I had two sisters that I knew of and who were close to the family at the time. One was open and kind, but I can't say if she accepted me. She was older and had her own things going on.

The younger one loved me. People always said I looked like her. She was and is always kind and loving to me—always present for me, no matter what. Whether I was Michael McCovery's child or not, she loved me.

Later in life, we found out that our father had fathered many other children. I actually have a closer relationship with what I believe is the youngest one. She doesn't care either. Whether it's been proven or not, she says, "We are family."

All those years, I never knew how much that affected me.

The one who loved me the most was my great-grandmother. She didn't care about the circumstances. She welcomed me, cared for me, and gave me memories of my father.

That was until my world shook—the day she could no longer recognize me.

After that, it was back to the darkness—back to being tolerated, back to shrinking myself so I wouldn't cause problems or be seen.

This all resurfaced in 2023. At that time, I was frustrated by how often abandonment was appearing in my life.

I didn't know back then that this was a form of abandonment I was experiencing. In fact, it felt like being unseen, unheard, or unsupported.

But as a kid, you don't have many rights—especially in a Black household or family. It was, "Do as I say," and "Respect your elders."

I didn't have the words for what I felt. I didn't really understand what was going on. I don't think the people around me grasped the ramifications of how they treated me.

It was just how people did things, and it was accepted behavior in the South.

Another layer of abandonment came from my mom—through inconsistent care, lack of affection, and unmet emotional needs.

Again, it was the way of the times, and I hold no grudges toward my mom. But it took time to heal and move forward.

One way I experienced inconsistent care was because my mom had to work all the time. As a single parent, she would leave us home alone for hours, with no one to look after us but ourselves.

At that time—and even while growing up—I didn't realize that this was a form of abandonment too. I just chalked it up to life.

She wasn't there physically, mentally, or emotionally. I was expected to push through and make it.

As a Black girl, I was expected not to cry, to show up strong, and to survive.

Abandonment trauma teaches the nervous system that connection is unsafe and unpredictable. So in adulthood, we either chase it, fear it, or shut down to avoid it altogether.

Remember, this is what was learned and stored in the Vault— the subconscious. Its job is to protect you and keep you from experiencing that pain ever again. However, it goes about it the wrong way.

This can look like chasing unavailable men.

What is an unavailable man, you ask—or unavailable people? This issue shows up in many areas, not just in relationships, but also in friendships, family, work, and home.

Let's start with: he's inconsistent. You can't depend on him; he isn't reliable. This triggers the part of abandonment rooted in inconsistent care or affection. This behavior feels familiar and acceptable because it replicates the unpredictability of childhood abandonment.

It's like when Dad says he's coming to get you for your birthday —but never shows up. It's broken promises left unhealed, unchecked, with no expectation for change or accountability.

Let's talk about the man who says all the right things but doesn't follow through.

You've never heard anyone say these things to you before, and you're just enamored. I know—while reading this comfortably—you might be thinking, "Yeah, this isn't me. I can't relate to this."

But let me bring it home.

It's when you tell yourself you're going to do something and then never follow through—or do something completely different. That frustration and disappointment in yourself come from not setting standards—which is why you also accept the same behavior from others.

Not having a father, not having someone to take care of you, not even having a safe space to say, "I want someone to take care of me," for fear of being judged—that can cause you to attract someone who sells you dreams with no destination.

This is where love-bombing begins—because he can see you've never had anyone say these kinds of things to you.

Then he slowly withdraws once you start expecting emotional intimacy.

He doesn't leave—because now the dynamics of the relationship have shifted. He's no longer doing anything, and he doesn't have to.

Do you know why?

Because you've taken over.

Now you're in appreciation and action mode. Now it's time to show him you deserve everything he said he could do or wants to do.

And now—you're trapped.

Because he never really had any intentions of doing anything. He just needed to see that he had you.

And because you were so needy and desperate to be taken care of, you fell for the okie-doke—and didn't wait for the proof to show up in his actions.

Because you've always taken care of everything, you were just okay with the thought of him doing something for you—even if he never actually did it.

No, sister.

It's definitely giving, "All I need is this, and I can do the rest."

If he can just be consistent with me...

If he can call me back...

If he can just buy me flowers...

Or just go to church with me...

That's good enough.

I already make the money. I can pay for the dates. I already have the car. I'm already successful.

All I need from him is to get some kind of job, and I'll handle the rest.

This is where women start to think, "If I can just get him to change this one thing, then I can work with him."

Not realizing that people only change when they want to. You can't make anyone do anything.

Let's do one more.

He doesn't define the relationship but wants to monopolize your time. He doesn't want you talking to other people and wants to "just go with the flow."

Ha!

RUUUN, GIRL... RUUUN!

This is a manipulation tactic.

He gets you emotionally involved—through sex, doing just enough to convince you, or by sharing vulnerable and intimate information to elicit your sympathy.

Then he gives you just enough to activate your abandonment wound—the little girl inside you starts to take over.

The proof is in the pudding:

• He dodges conversations about commitment.
• He plays on your emotions by gaslighting you.
• He makes everything your fault.

• He never takes accountability for his actions.

See, women date potential. Men date for the present.

When women date based on potential—rather than seeing a man for who he truly is—we get caught up in fixing, tolerating, and hoping.

At the end of the day, we're the ones at fault.

Why? Because, often, that man didn't even sell you potential—you sold it to yourself.

You told yourself lies about what you wanted it to be so it could fit—instead of seeing it for what it was and deciding whether you actually wanted to move forward.

Some reasons for this can vary.

But one major reason?

Our nervous system.

It likes what's familiar because it believes familiar is safe. We know how to handle someone abandoning us—we've done this before. This start-over-and-try-again cycle.

So because of that, we're not choosing from our healed, loved, and abundant selves.

We're choosing from the wounded little girl inside who's still looking for what she didn't receive.

Unhealed abandonment wounds teach that love is:

• Conditional
• Inconsistent
• Withheld when you need reciprocity

These wounds manifest as behaviors. They become personality traits. And it doesn't just stop, as you might think.

It doesn't go away just because you grow up.

It becomes who you are now. You just act it out in adult relationships—searching for what you lacked in childhood… in grown-up bodies.

The mind and body feel safe with what's familiar. That's why you're attracted to certain people. That's why it becomes your type.

Yes—what you've been through ultimately shapes what you pursue, attract, and believe.

You only believe you can get what you feel worthy of in dating.

You date at the level of your self-esteem.

And you live at the level of your perspective.

Let's shift this next part to rejection and how it can also influence your partner choices. Because the abandonment wound was never healed, it creates a need to earn love to avoid rejection. The more I can give, do, and show, the less likely I am to be turned down or overlooked. But is that really true?

As we delve into this topic, let's discuss the hyper-independent, type-A personality, loyal-to-dysfunction woman. Yes, I know that was a blow, but breathe through it and let's move forward. Yes, it's Black girl magic and the therapist Monique is coming for your throat.

That hyper-independence isn't a personality trait, baby girl; it's a protective strategy. Like me, you didn't just wake up one day and decide to be superwoman, to handle it all—no, this was necessary. To prevent pain, to avoid becoming like your mother, to ensure your kids don't go without—you had to become this hyper-independent woman to survive. You became super self-reliant because you made an unspoken contract with yourself: you would never be played like this again, or hurt like this again.

So you took matters into your own hands. You didn't choose to be this way; you had to be. No one was there, no one came, no one noticed or even asked why. All we hear is "Black women are mad, angry, too independent, not soft or feminine," but no one is asking the question why.

However, the demands on the Black woman didn't change. You're still needed to keep it together. You're still expected to take care of everything and to show up and save the day—yeah, that hasn't changed.

So we learn to survive and adapt. But how does this affect the way we date and who we choose?

Let me break it down for you.

Because you moved in this manner, you've projected the image that you have it all together, that you don't need anybody, and don't require any help. Even though you and I both know that's a big, bold-faced lie. If someone could help us and had the means to do so, we would want it—but would we accept it?

This is where our words say one thing, and our behavior says another. This is why we often choose those who need help and support—because it makes us feel safe, wanted, and let's not forget: needed. We are praised for our hard work, respected and celebrated for our resilience—all the while setting ourselves up to accept bread-crumbs. If we didn't prove our worth, we would trigger the abandonment wound and feel unworthy, or think, "This is not how it works." It contradicts everything I learned about receiving love as a child.

This leads us to choose someone with whom we can prove our worth because it validates the narrative in our heads that productivity equals love.

So we don't need him to have it all together. Why, you ask? Because we already do—all we need is a man, and for that man to stay. We pay for the dates by slipping him the card, even though our name or business name is on it and the waitress can see that I am paying the bill—but for his pride, we do it anyway.

We have conditioned ourselves to believe that the only thing missing in life is a man. That we have it all together—that is, on paper—and the only thing stopping us from appearing even better are the "Why are you single?" questions at the family cookout. "Where's your man?" "There must be something wrong with you." "Oh, you can't keep a man?" "You're going to be alone with a dog, and then no one will want you."

So, you kick it into overdrive, trying not to reach 40 without a husband. You tell yourself there must be a method to this. "What am I missing? Why haven't I cracked the code? All my life, I've achieved everything I needed through hard work and perseverance —why doesn't this work for me? What's wrong with me? I need to work harder; I need to give more. Maybe if I dated a guy who made significantly less than me, I wouldn't appear to have something wrong with me."

So you settle. With that settling, you accept the idea that this man will never show up for you—and that is okay, because you've got it. "I've got it, me and him, because that is what I signed up for."

You don't realize that this is a trauma response. You haven't seen that, because no one had you as a kid, you learned to rely on yourself. Because you weren't seen and were ignored, you became a target for abuse—and as a result, you ensure you are seen by never trusting anyone and never being with someone you can't protect yourself from.

All your decisions about whom to choose were shaped by experiences you did not heal from. You became the one who over-gave, over-apologized to save relationships, and transformed into a chameleon to fix things. You shrank yourself and denounced your own work ethics, codes, and standards to reduce the shame of being in your late 30s without even a potential backup for marriage.

Reflecting on some of the expressions discussed in the last chapter, you may have reached a place where your mind forgets the rejection, but your body is activated and now in hyper-fix-it mode because you can't endure another failed situationship.

Since I've mentioned it a few times, let's briefly discuss self-sabotaging behavior.

What is self-sabotage? It's any behavior that is harmful or potentially harmful to yourself. It can manifest as negative self-talk, holding onto limiting beliefs, trying to control everything, and comparing yourself to others. Yes, that is self-sabotaging behavior.

But let's bring it closer to home. It's when you see a guy who is everything you want, but you won't talk to him or even allow yourself to be approached because you've already deemed yourself unworthy—so you leave the room. It's when someone tries to give you something (e.g., a compliment), and you respond with negative remarks about yourself to stop them because you don't want to feel embarrassed by the compliment—like saying, "Oh, this outfit? I actually feel like a busted can of biscuits."

Self-sabotage is more than just behavior—it stems from low self-esteem and how you perceive yourself. It's also a trauma response. It comes from childhood, where you learned, "If I do it first, I can soften the blow." This gives you a sense of control. It's a defense mechanism to protect yourself from harm: "I will hurt myself before they do," or "I will leave before they leave me."

On one hand, you don't even try because you've deemed yourself unworthy; on the other hand, it's a defense mechanism. It's a way of playing small and keeping yourself small. You see, if you don't go after what you want, it can't hurt you. In fact, what's the point? You might as well stay in this lane, do what you can, and never hope again.

It's when you are being loved correctly, but you do something to sabotage it because your mind says, "If they can stay through this, they must be able to handle hard times"—not realizing that this logic doesn't add up and is only coming from a place of pain and fear.

Unhealed abandonment wounds create unhealed core beliefs and narratives, which lead to behaviors intended to protect you. This results in behaviors like self-sabotage, settling, and cycles of disappointment. This is not due to the woman being weak or foolish, but because she hasn't healed the parts of herself that were abandoned.

Your brain is doing what brains do: thinking. It runs through scenario after scenario to determine which story will play out. Then it responds—without learning—because the goal is to protect.

This is where the sabotage begins. At first, it doesn't feel like that. You are absolutely clueless and believe what you are doing makes sense. It feels like protection, so you avoid the big things but engage in little subtle actions. You start off small. For instance, you may not answer when he calls, pull back more, or give him the silent treatment. Then you may play little pranks to test his tolerance level —like saying, "I can't have kids because of some illness," or "I was told that I have a condition that can't be cured but isn't contagious," etc., to see how he responds and if he can handle it.

Ultimately, this behavior ends up destroying the relationship in some ways. It causes you to over-give or overcompensate for fear that you've gone too far and need him to stay or make amends. You often ghost them before they can reject you. You find reasons not to like him—which isn't hard because your thinking tends to be negative. You become hyper-independent because needing people feels too risky.

For a long time, disappointment was your trigger. You would expect things without communicating this, leading to disappointment—and in some cases, you did it on purpose to validate your belief that they would leave. You intentionally picked unavailable men because you knew, in the end, they wouldn't be enough—and this confirmed the core belief and narrative you held about yourself and dating.

This led to subtle self-abandonment all in the name of protection. You knowingly fell for emotionally unavailable partners because it felt safer than real intimacy.

Nobody wants to talk about how hard it is to transition from unhealthy to healthy. The times you have to call yourself out on your behaviors and reasoning can be daunting. It's scary to be in the unknown and learn to trust. It's easy to argue about not answering phone calls, but it's hard to confront why you cave in and isolate. It's challenging when a healthy person chooses themselves because your unhealed behaviors could cause them pain—and they explain this to you…ugh!

Let's discuss some common self-sabotaging behaviors linked to abandonment. One I mentioned earlier is testing love: "Will he stay if I push him away?" Another would be avoiding good love because it doesn't match the struggle you're accustomed to; falling for emotionally unavailable partners; or clinging tightly or ghosting quickly.

We often say things like "protecting my peace" to justify bad or unhealed behavior, but what we're really doing is protecting the wound. Because if I don't let anyone in, no one can hurt me.

The funny part is we get right back out there to date, marry, and try again, without realizing that the core belief, narrative, and unhealed wound are telling us what to do, how to do it, who to date, and how to date.

Next, let's discuss emotional dysregulation that causes abandonment fear and anxious behaviors. Abandonment fear is the worry about someone leaving or rejecting you. This fear can be so overwhelming that it leads to anxiety or anxious behaviors—physically, mentally, and/or emotionally. It can manifest as insecurities, causing one to be clingy or "needy," seeking excessive reassurance and often finding it difficult to trust others.

If not careful, this fear of abandonment can make the fear of being abandoned come true due to toxic and unhealed behaviors— i.e., self-sabotaging, being hyper-vigilant, etc., as discussed earlier.

Certain triggers can activate the abandonment wound and wire the nervous system to expect abandonment, thus kicking off anxious or fearful behaviors. For instance, if a partner doesn't answer their phone, fails to keep their word, or ghosts and then returns, this can send the nervous system into fight, flight, fawn, or freeze. This can manifest as:

• **Fight Mode**: Hyper-vigilance in relationships ("What did that text mean?")

• **Flight Mode**: Escaping intimacy by staying busy, detached, or emotionally unavailable.

• **Freeze Mode:** Feeling paralyzed when it's time to speak up or connect

• **Fawn Mode:** People-pleasing, overfunctioning, and care-taking to stay "wanted"

Fear isn't always visible; it often lurks beneath the surface, fueled by the subconscious and trauma. It dictates how our bodies respond —or fail to respond. Our bodies become warning signs, signaling when love feels safe or unsafe based on the information stored within. This is emotional dysregulation, which can make it challenging to make sound decisions while under stress or feeling threatened. The body reacts as if every situation is dramatic—sometimes with intensity or withdrawal—making it difficult to leave someone, even when that person poses a danger.

You're not bipolar; it's simply your body trying to protect you from abandonment, yet struggling to prioritize your own needs.

Fear of abandonment leads you to overanalyze texts, tones, and behaviors, always on the lookout for signs of trouble to brace yourself for potential ghosting or rejection. Another anxious behavior may involve seeking constant reassurance—much like the little girl on TikTok who repeatedly asks, "You love me? You love me?" and receives affirmations from her father.

This manifests as clinging tightly when someone pulls away, panicking when someone requests space, or interpreting another person's distant behavior as a personal rejection or a precursor to being ghosted.

Coping strategies often emerge in an attempt to maintain the relationship, striving to eliminate fear. This can involve using intimacy to strengthen the bond, controlling behaviors, over-functioning, people-pleasing, and hypervigilance.

Station 4

Stuff Him Up

What's Really Inside That Bear You Built

Τhis station peels back the layers of the "bae-r" you've built the version of love you've created to feel safe, seen, or needed. Often, that bae-r is stuffed with people-pleasing, codependency, and emotional over-functioning.

When abandonment wounds go unhealed, love turns into performance. You start fixing, overgiving, and shrinking to keep someone close. Your happiness becomes tangled in their moods, choices, and validation.

Here, you'll begin to ask: What am I really filling this relationship with? And more importantly what am I emptying in myself to do it?

* * *

Some behaviors that reveal abandonment wounds in our adult lives include people-pleasing and codependency. So, what exactly are people-pleasing and codependent behaviors? Codependency occurs when your identity, self-worth, and emotional safety depend on someone else. Essentially, you feel good only when they are good. This often leads to over-functioning or fixing—both aspects of people-pleasing—and losing yourself to maintain a relationship. Your joy, life, and happiness hinge on the feelings, actions, or approval of another person.

Due to trauma, codependent behaviors frequently stem from abandonment wounds. These behaviors serve as a protective response against rejection. Often masked as loyalty, commitment, and sacrifice, they are actually forms of emotional enmeshment, where your needs are overshadowed by someone else's. You may find yourself thinking, "As long as she's happy, I'm happy," or expressing, "I like making other people happy," without realizing it comes at your own expense.

People-pleasing is the twin sister of codependency. It involves doing things to please others even when you don't want to or when it doesn't feel right. Often, individuals compromise their morals, values, and boundaries to maintain relationships, driven by the fear that the person they are pleasing—or are codependent on—will leave, thus triggering the abandonment wound.

People-pleasing can manifest as:

- Avoiding conflict at all costs
- Feeling responsible for others' emotions
- Needing affirmation or validation to feel "enough"

Like self-sabotage, people-pleasing is a trauma response. It's a defense mechanism for those who grew up believing that love must be earned, managed, or performed. The objective of both codependency and people-pleasing is self-neglect for the sake of the relationship, aiming to prevent the core beliefs or narratives formed by the abandonment wound.

Ultimately, all of this is an attempt to protect the inner child from experiencing the pain once felt during childhood—or at any stage of life when the trauma occurred. Self-neglect becomes the new norm and can evolve into self-abandonment. This often begins in childhood when love is conditional—based on behavior, performance, or silence.

Self-neglect can look like:

- Feeling guilty for taking time for yourself
- Ignoring your own physical, emotional, and mental pain for the sake of others
- Believing that self-care is selfish and self-centered

At this time, you may not have any boundaries. If you're an AA female like me, growing up in a Black home often meant there were no boundaries. It was commonly understood and frequently expressed with phrases like, "You do as I say, not as I do," and "This is my house; if you don't like it, you can leave." Physical punishment for perceived disrespect was also a norm.

As a result, you may have no clear understanding of what boundaries are. You might believe that loyalty is synonymous with self-sacrifice, and that this is normal. If you questioned this belief, you may have been taught, punished, or even preached into submission—such as with the admonition, "Children, obey your parents" —without realizing that this scripture applies to children, not to you as a full-grown woman, possibly with kids and a husband. Yet, the fear remains that if you don't comply with their wishes, they will abandon you, cut you off, or ostracize you.

Whether this threat is real or not, it feels very real to you, perpetuating a cycle of people-pleasing and performance. You lose sight of who you are or who you could become. Your identity becomes theirs to shape, and you shape-shift to maintain peace, reduce conflict, and keep your partner comfortable, all to avoid confrontation.

As a result, you shrink. You bury your feelings deep inside. You even wear a mask to hide your true emotions—this is known as masking—just to avoid losing them. In the process, you are losing yourself. You might tell yourself, "I am the bigger person," but in reality, you are the unhealed person. You abandon yourself, allowing their identity to become yours. You become enmeshed.

You may feel disoriented, unsure of your own direction, which leaves you feeling empty, lost, and even more alone—the very thing you fought so hard not to be: alone, left behind, rejected, or abandoned. The question is: Are you loving them at the cost of losing yourself?

Let's discuss attachment and attachment theory. Attachment theory, developed by John Bowlby and later expanded by Mary Ainsworth, explains how bonds formed in childhood affect one's life. These bonds shape the way we connect with others and are especially significant in dating and other forms of relationships.

Due to experiences such as abandonment, inconsistency, or emotional neglect in childhood, we develop attachment styles that prioritize survival over safety. This is crucial because it marks the beginning of our emotional patterns. The interactions we had—or lacked—during our upbringing caused trauma, which shaped our core beliefs and narratives, instilling a fear of abandonment. This fear then drives behaviors that perpetuate a cycle of running from something we are ultimately creating ourselves.

When one's foundation is unstable, they seek to establish their own sense of security, often building attachments to partners based on their fears. Let's briefly overview the different attachment styles.

The first is Anxious Attachment, characterized by the core belief: If I do something wrong, you will leave me, so I must people-please and stay close to feel safe. This belief leads to a fear of partners pulling away, prompting behaviors such as overanalyzing conversations, tones, and scenarios in one's mind to ensure safety in the relationship. This often results in attraction to emotionally unavailable or inconsistent partners, mistaking anxiety for chemistry and access for love. Consequently, individuals become accustomed to receiving only crumbs of attention and affection.

Next is Avoidant Attachment, whose core belief is: I can't get too close because only bad things happen when I do, so I must give a little and hide a little. People with this attachment style are emotionally distant, struggle to communicate their needs, lack emotional intelligence, feel smothered by intimacy, and avoid vulnerability at all costs. Their mindset is that if they can build someone up, it creates a safe space for that person—someone they can fix—rather than allowing someone to see through their own pain or trusting them with it. This results in emotional disconnection and the very fears they harbor—being alone due to lack of connection—become scarier than the prospect of being truly loved.

The next attachment style is Disorganized (Fearful-Avoidant) Attachment, characterized by the core belief: "I want love, but it's not safe." This describes many people. We are often taught to seek and desire love, as if we don't already possess it. We chase something that is inherently within us, but due to our abandonment wounds, we fail to recognize our own worth. Consequently, we pursue something we fear.

This attachment style combines elements of anxious clinging and avoidant shutting down. Individuals with this attachment style feel that life cannot continue without love, yet they fear it deeply. They often find themselves in chaotic relationships, drawn to toxic partners, believing that love is validated if the person stays. They frequently repeat cycles of toxic, addictive, or confusing love dynamics. Their belief is: "I can build a partner I can control because real love feels dangerous." This shifts their core belief to: "My love language is survival," in which they create their own battleground, manage their battle wounds, and persist until they get it right.

In the next section, we will shift our focus to choosing love with clarity—recognizing the patterns that keep us stuck and learning how to pursue relationships that honor our healing. I want you to reach a place where you can identify your patterns and recognize those that no longer serve you. As we discussed earlier, trauma can distort the lens through which you view relationships. Unhealed abandonment wounds can make you perceive survival as intimacy when, in reality, it is a trauma bond.

I want to address why so many Black women feel trapped in relationships that resemble survival. When you are grappling with abandonment wounds, there is a false high associated with being chosen. Because of your past experiences of abandonment, being chosen feels like gold. Finally, someone sees me, and I don't have to change, or finally someone picked me from all the others, and I finally have someone. This mindset often leads individuals to mistake this dynamic for love when it is, in fact, an expression of unhealed trauma.

Being picked—even by someone who is not healthy for you— can make the unhealed version of you feel seen, valued, and safe. While you may feel relieved initially, you often drop your boundaries to avoid losing that person because they chose you. You stay, even when your body and nervous system signal red flags—warning signs of unsafe or anxious behavior. Yet, because being chosen feels better than being alone, you ignore these signals and label it as chemistry. You mistake attention for affection and possession for protection, leading you to associate being picked or chosen with being valued.

Let's be clear: there is nothing wrong with wanting to be chosen; we all desire that. However, when choosing with clarity, you must understand that you are already chosen, you have already been picked, and you don't need to downplay yourself to gain someone's approval. It's like a little level of Delu-Lu until what you truly desire comes to you. If you walk and act as if you're broken, adopting a scarcity mindset, you will make choices that reflect that. Conversely, if you walk in abundance and believe that you are enough and have everything you need, you will make decisions based on your true worth rather than lack.

I know it may take time for you to receive, believe, and practice this, but it starts with your perception. Let's begin by identifying what something truly is, doing so in real time and out loud. One must cultivate emotional intelligence—awareness of one's feelings— and then confront these feelings, acknowledging the need for change.

Let's start with what it means to be cherished. Personally, I once believed that being chosen was everything. I was always trying to outshine others, thinking that being selected over someone else made me "that girl" and top tier. This mindset reflects a troubling aspect of our community today: Black women often feel the need to one-up one another, sometimes over a man. While there are many factors contributing to this mindset, that is a topic for another book.

To be cherished is more than merely being liked or appreciated; it is an action that unfolds in real time. It means being seen, loved, and valued through intentional behavior that reflects what is important to you. I know, it sounds profound, right? Take a moment to visualize this for yourself. Imagine being in a space where you are not just loved, but truly cherished. Picture someone who holds you dear, where every action they take is motivated by a desire to protect and prioritize your well-being because you matter to them. You truly matter to them. Everything they do is influenced by their consideration for you.

As a child raised in an inconsistent, unpredictable household, you may have developed an anxious attachment style, causing you to associate emotional intensity with intimacy. In some cases, chaos becomes your new normal, and calm can feel suspicious. This is where we discussed self-sabotaging behaviors and the various ways they manifest.

We learn that love is something we must chase, earn, prove, or fix to avoid falling apart. This creates a pattern of abandonment, leading to anxiety when things go too well, as discussed in the previous chapter. It's essential to pay attention to your body—what messages is it sending you?

Remember, even safe and healthy relationships can be triggering. You must take the time to reflect on each incident in real time. Additionally, you need to understand what safe and secure love looks like. Challenge your thoughts—specifically, your core beliefs and narratives—and ask yourself: do you genuinely want to be loved?

Hold yourself accountable by asking questions like, "Hey, you say one thing but do another. What's going on?" This is the moment to investigate which parts of you may be deceiving you. Is it your mind, body, emotions, or perhaps your subconscious? After that, seek to understand the underlying reasons why.

Oftentimes, we as women make decisions based on our emotions, which can lead to confusion between the chemistry of chaos and love. Due to our body's makeup, trauma causes us to crave that adrenaline rush. Have you ever felt like it was just too calm? Or found yourself drawn to toxicity? That is trauma at work; it craves the high, and without it—can it even be love?

The hot and cold texts, the love bombs, the emotional ups and downs, the arguments, and the passionate sex—these are all aspects of a toxic relationship. It's not uncommon for someone to attract the opposite in trauma. For example, if you have an anxious attachment style, you might feel uneasy when things are too calm and start engaging in behaviors you believe will keep you safe. As a result, you attract and date someone with an avoidant attachment style, who fears closeness and pulls back.

This creates a push-and-pull dynamic, triggering each other without even realizing it. The adrenaline rises, making it feel like passion because that's what you've learned. It's also familiar, leading you to confuse inconsistency with excitement, and you may believe that this overwhelming pull is love—when it's really just your attachment wounds flaring up.

Let's discuss how to choose from a healed place. What does that look like? It looks like no longer asking or begging anyone to be in your life. It's not about "Anyone want to buy a heart?" (a reference to K. Michelle's album), but rather coming from a place of abundance. It means no longer sidelining yourself, your feelings, your goals, and what's important to you for a date, support, affection, or out of fear of never having anyone. It's about stopping self-abandonment, cherishing yourself, and moving with intention.

There are signs of growth—such as how you perceive situations and how your body reacts. You find yourself asking questions instead of simply reacting out of emotion. You date wisely, considering your own needs, and take your time to discover what truly matters to you, knowing that there is time and no longer living in fear. You don't mistake stillness for boredom or feel it as abandonment. You learn to regulate your emotions and allow yourself the space to feel them. You transition from a state of adrenaline to one of peace, realizing that gentle love is more fulfilling than seeking validation through love. You no longer require chaos to feel seen, alive, or worthy.

You find yourself not checking your phone, no longer anxious for the next text or interaction. You establish boundaries and understand what standards are, recognizing the bar you set for yourself. If you lack standards or boundaries, you learn to create them. This is the space of healing. You no longer betray your own needs to maintain connection. Safe and nurturing love becomes appealing rather than dull. You stop idolizing survival love and no longer date for potential. Instead, you date for what is, seeing reality clearly and making conscious decisions based on the information at hand. You no longer wait for or attempt to fix someone to meet your needs— you already possess everything you require. In fact, the answer lies within you. You are both the need and the solution.

You no longer view loneliness as a trigger. Your core beliefs have transformed. You see being single and fulfilled as a more desirable goal than being coupled and unfulfilled. It's important to clarify that this isn't a critique of relationships or the desire for one; it's an acknowledgment that a relationship isn't everything. This mindset can lead to confusion and further heartbreak, as you may believe that entering a relationship will resolve all your issues.

So, how do you choose from a place of clarity rather than pain? You must create an internal blueprint. Understand your abandonment wounds and limiting beliefs. Redefine love from a healthier perspective. Ask yourself: Would love treat me this way? Would love abandon me? Am I viewing this situation through a lens of hurt or love? What are my needs in this moment?

Redefining love means embracing a love that doesn't involve self-sacrifice, a love that is not about merely surviving or shrinking. It's important to recognize that other changes may be necessary as well, particularly regarding your friends and family. I had to come to terms with the fact that I couldn't rely on others' words of encouragement. The reason was simple: I didn't want a marriage like theirs. I wanted to be cared for, treated gently, and cherished. What I observed around me were many women marrying because it was expected of them. For them, marriage provided security and a voice, making them feel important. I had to realize that I already possessed those qualities and consciously ignore external influences, refusing to let their words take root in my heart. I understood that this journey might be lonely and challenging because I didn't simply want to be married.

Consequently, I decided to limit my conversations about my experiences and desires and sought out people who were living the kind of marriage I envisioned. But first, I needed to identify what that vision entailed. Becoming a trailblazer is no small feat. It required many nights of tears, embarrassment, and the fear that my dreams might never come true. It also demanded the courage to forge a new path.

I once heard a girl on TikTok say, "Imagine trying to break generational curses while still seeking approval from the generation that is cursed." This insight struck me profoundly. It felt like an explosion in my heart, mind, and soul, clearing away the old world and laying the groundwork for the new.

Perspective and perception became the new lens through which I viewed life. I began challenging my beliefs and observations. I altered my algorithm to focus on podcasts that aligned with my aspirations—specifically, dating and marriage. However, I had to endure hardship and break free from survival mode to reach a place where I could examine my habits and initiate change. I then began working on my self-esteem, understanding that no matter what I did, if I didn't believe in myself, I could not truly receive what I desired.

Because most Black women are conditioned to settle, I had to work on my mindset—my sense of worth—and recognize that I could have the kind of relationship and marriage I desired. I realized that love and being cherished were normal, not just for those who worked for it.

When I saw on Instagram that there were men who washed their partners' hair, cooked for them, and did thoughtful things for them, it broke another chain within me. I thought, "You mean to tell me there are people who are bigger than me in committed relationships, and they are just being themselves?!" It was an explosive realization. Everything started to come together, but first came the awareness.

I began creating boundaries and embracing change, which led to continuous growth. I accepted that yesterday's price is not today's price. Why? Because every day, I was working on myself—my self-development, self-esteem, self-worth, and identity—constantly changing and evolving.

I no longer lived by blind hope; I lived by action. For instance, I always wanted to be the type of woman who wore heels. This shift came from distancing myself from people who influenced my identity and were comfortable with the version of me they knew, rather than supporting the version I aspired to become. I started creating folders on my phone with images of the woman I wanted to be and how she would dress. Now, I am that woman, and the next step is wearing heels.

I struggled with walking in heels for long periods, so I tried various numbing creams recommended on TikTok and researched ways to alleviate pain in the balls of my feet on YouTube. I also moved my little moped treadmill upstairs to make it easier to use. I applied a technique called habit stacking, where you integrate a new habit into something you already do. Since I often listened to podcasts and sermons online, I started doing that while walking in heels to help me stay goal-oriented.

To be successful, you must create an environment conducive to your goals. This realization made things easier for me. However, I later recognized that losing weight was my ultimate objective. When I vocalized this, I realized it was all about shifting my weight to the balls of my feet—and then it clicked. The burden wouldn't be as heavy if I began taking better care of myself and improving my eating habits. Since I was secretly dissatisfied with my life and being single, I struggled to cope. I engaged in overworking and neglected my emotional and mental well-being, all while trying to embody the strong Black woman stereotype.

As a therapist, you might expect me to practice what I preach. Yet, as I mentioned earlier, I was unaware of many of these insights while navigating life as a single parent in survival mode. Now that my daughter is 20, I have gained clarity about my struggles, and this awareness has empowered me to apply my skills and embrace change—hence, the motivation to write this book.

I focused on understanding my dating patterns, creating worksheets and charts to help identify my standards, morals, and values. These evolved as I did. What mattered during my unhealed abandonment wounds became irrelevant in the healed version of myself. It was time to walk the talk and truly believe in my journey. Though I occasionally faltered—which is normal—I was dismantling deeply ingrained belief systems from my childhood that I needed to relearn in adulthood.

I had to understand what emotional safety meant and create it for myself. I needed to discover who I am and what works for me, establishing new patterns, eating habits, and lifestyles. I transformed my identity from the "strong Black woman who has it all" to simply being a woman. I learned that this was enough, and I could choose to embrace other aspects of myself that resonated with who I wanted to be.

I made myself the priority and asked: Am I trying to maintain relationships, or am I doing this out of fear? Before accepting anything, I created routines that helped me stay grounded in clarity —choosing what's best for me time and again. I focused on dating, waiting, and living a healed life.

I no longer ask anyone if they want to buy a heart.

In fact, it's no longer for sale.

Station 5

Dress Him

When Love Is Just a Costume for Survival

In this station, we uncover how love becomes another performance, another survival role wrapped in strength. For many Black women, love isn't something received with ease; it's something earned through labor, loyalty, and silence.

You'll explore how you were taught to build a partner, cover his flaws, and dress him up to look like love while your own needs stayed buried. This chapter reveals how the "strong Black woman" script often asks you to settle, sacrifice, and survive in costumes that hide your softness.

Here, we begin unlearning. Because you were never meant to be his stylist, savior, or shield, you were meant to be seen.

* * *

Black women in America have been taught to "make it work," even at a cost. This often comes at the expense of their peace, purpose, and power.

Let's discuss where I learned to build instead of receive.

For far too long, Black women have been quietly conditioned to build. This expectation is rooted in our history, childhood, culture, and even our church communities. We are expected to hold everything together. Being labeled a strong Black woman is often seen as a medal and an honor, while failing to meet this expectation can lead to being called "too emotional," "weak," or "selfish." The role of a strong Black woman comes with unrealistic expectations, often leading to being used and abused. It sets a standard for women to go above and beyond while accepting self-sacrifice.

The church plays a significant role in this conditioning, with high expectations for women to prioritize church duties over home responsibilities, often facing scorn when things fall apart at home. The belief is that if you give to the church, surely God will take care of you and your family.

We've witnessed women trying to fix broken men, enduring abuse, and sacrificing their own needs so their children can eat, all while the man is glorified. Growing up, we saw women make do, survive, and tolerate inconsistency in relationships, often justifying poor behavior with excuses like "He's just a man," or "Boys will be boys," teaching women to accept such treatment.

Messages like "That's a good man, Savannah, and he's just going through a tough time" (a reference to *Waiting to Exhale*) illustrate how we have been taught to tolerate unacceptable behaviors under the guise of loyalty, with the underlying belief that we'll never find better, that we don't deserve more, and that no one else will want us at this stage in our lives.

We are often expected to support our partners until they get back on their feet, but this comes at our own expense. It's as if we are not deemed worthy of reciprocity or good treatment. For Black women, that luxury often feels unattainable. To earn love, we feel we must endure struggle and suffering to prove our worth.

Malcolm X famously said:

"The most disrespected person in America is the Black woman. The most unprotected person in America is the Black woman. The most neglected person in America is the Black woman."

I wonder why that is. But that's a discussion for another book.

Black woman, see yourself in this narrative, and evolve. The world has fought hard to steal our voice, rights, and strength. We embody these qualities, but we are also so much more.

We don't have to work for love; it is already ours. Whether acknowledged or not, it was given to us at birth.

It is not your responsibility to change or heal someone else. You are more than that, and once you stop trying to fix and care for others, you can redirect that energy into yourself, creating the space and momentum to become what you were truly meant to be...

Greatness.

Let's explore the cycle of these relationships a bit more. Below is a five-stage pattern, the emotional cycle in codependent or trauma-bonded relationships:

- Stage 1: Attraction to Potential → Driven by anxious attachment and codependency (Beattie, LePera) ("He just needs someone to believe in him")

- Stage 2: Overfunctioning → Family systems theory (Lerner) (You become his motivator, mother, and manager)

- Stage 3: Resentment → Codependency burnout (Beattie, Lerner) (You feel depleted, unseen, and unheard)

- Stage 4: Emotional Crash → Trauma bond collapse (Carnes, Thomas) (You stay longer, hoping he'll finally understand)

- Stage 5: Grief and Self-Blame → Recovery stages post-toxic relationship (Thomas) (Wondering if you were the problem)

So what does this look like in real time?

Consider a woman who meets a man on a dating app—let's say Tinder. Initially, things are going well. He fits her ideal in terms of physical attributes and communicates his emotions effectively. However, after three months, communication dwindles—he calls less frequently, and text responses become slow.

She enters fix-it mode, trying to discern what he needs so she can provide it. She thinks, "Surely he will come back, and we'll be like we were before." He mentions he's stressed about buying a house, and since she's gone through the process twice, she feels equipped to help him. She goes into overdrive to prove her worth.

But nothing changes. He remains distant, delaying responses to her texts until the next day, then two days later. Anxiety and fear begin to creep in; she feels unseen, undervalued, and alone. Old feelings of abandonment resurface.

Then she spirals.

She pushes even harder, convincing herself he's just experiencing a tough time and that he's a good man, so she holds on as she was taught. She stays longer, hoping he will recognize her efforts and miss her because she has invested so much energy and time into him. Yet, she realizes she may have rushed into things. Now, she feels herself crashing, replaying the scenario repeatedly, questioning what she did wrong. She wonders what more she could have given, feeling depleted and unreciprocated.

An ache settles in her heart and stomach.

Suddenly, everything she has been avoiding and fighting against rushes in like a whirlwind, tearing apart everything in its path.

She remains in this relationship, believing that if she does enough, he will stay. She builds and builds, seeking emotional security, often dating men who are beneath her means, convinced she can control the situation.

But then the worst happens.

The man who has less than her leaves, abandoning her.

This deepens her despair, forcing her to either sink or swim. She either begins to question why this happened or blames herself, wondering what she did wrong, so she can try harder next time.

Thoughts like "I have to be needed to be kept" lead her to seek out partners who have less than the last one, even at the cost of her self-esteem, just to avoid being alone.

This forced potential incurs costs that you may not recognize now, but in the future, you will see that it cost you your dreams. It has placed you in survival mode and unhealthy relationships. It has led to emotional burnout and misalignment in your life, putting you on a leash of desperation for love, making you willing to do anything to obtain it. There is a void that needs to be filled, and until it is filled with the right things, it will become insatiable.

Helping others becomes your identity as you try to fill this void. The high of being needed and useful is an attempt to satisfy an insatiable hunger. Fixing others is masked by the ideal of the strong Black woman—that it is your duty to fix, to hold space, and to care for others—because if not, what are you doing? It defines your worth, and if you don't fix things, you may feel you have no value. You fix so you won't become invisible, powerless, or abandoned.

Fixing causes you to forget your own problems. You become so distracted or entrenched in survival mode that you fail to realize it all begins with you. It's difficult to see that you are not truly trying to fix others, but rather attempting to fill your own unmet needs.

Have you ever noticed how hard it is to slow down and sit in silence?

Yes, it's because it's scary, uncomfortable, hard, and lonely.

Until you address the void, you won't feel safe within yourself—enough to be single and okay with it. You will find yourself in relationships out of fear of being alone. Avoidance is not a healthy response or coping mechanism; it is a trauma response. By not slowing down, remaining in survival mode, and staying distracted, you perpetuate the unhealthy cycle of abandonment wounds, which ultimately keeps you dating the same type of person.

Avoidance isn't just about shutting down or walking away; it is, as I mentioned, staying busy to avoid feeling. It can also involve recognizing your patterns and still choosing unavailable partners to evade the work of healing your abandonment wounds. It is a detachment from what you truly want and deserve. It manifests as emotional numbness, masked as strength, and involves ghosting accountability, reflection, or therapy. Avoidance may feel like control, as if you have the upper hand, but in reality, it is fear disguised.

Let's talk about potential.

What does it mean?

How am I doing this?

Well, let's get started.

Potential means having or showing the capacity to become or develop into something in the future. This is the essence of the book —The Build-A-BAE-R Syndrome!

Women date for potential, while men date for the present moment. This is why we often feel disappointed—because we don't fall in love with who they are, but with who they could be.

This is why it hurts so much and is difficult for us to believe that he could ever treat us this way—because we never saw him for who he truly is, but for who we hoped he could become. Not only that, we envisioned who we wanted him to be and what we wanted the relationship to become.

This need, desperation, and scarcity mindset can lead someone to sacrifice self-worth, safety, and identity, as they are blinded by these emotions.

This is DANGEROUS!

You see, the red flags were already present—you simply chose not to see them. It wasn't him who lied to you; it was you who lied to yourself. Because you wanted it so badly, you ignored the signs— the signs of another woman, his dangerous temper, and his unreliability.

Because of the strong Black woman gene, along with everything seemingly falling into place when you set your mind to it, you thought this situation would be the same.

This can keep you trapped in a loop because we, as Black women, are often hardheaded, resilient, and stubborn. We try to prove people wrong and even prove ourselves wrong. But in the end, we learn the hard way—you can't make anyone change.

People change because they want to—due to trauma, religion, or hardship.

At this stage in life, we are who we are, and most people are not truly trying to change for the better. Change often occurs only when a person reaches their breaking point and realizes something must give.

Because of this potential, desperation, and fear of running out of time, you fall in love with fragments—pieces of a puzzle—trying to decipher a grown man's behavior and words, even though he doesn't know how to communicate or has no desire to learn.

You internalize all of this, thinking you are not good enough and that you should do more.

So, you go into overdrive again—to save this man and mold him into what you want him to be so that you don't have to be alone, or to avoid the future your family predicted for you (i.e., becoming a lonely cat lady), or to avoid working on yourself.

You must learn the difference between healthy encouragement, enabling, and overfunctioning.

There was a saying I heard on Instagram:

"Potential is what you see in others that you would do in that situation."

I believe this to be true—because if not, why would we try so hard to change outcomes, give, or fix? It's because it reflects what we would want someone to do for us and what we would do if we were in that situation.

This is a trap, and we must be careful to monitor our motivations. Slow down and bring light to the situation. At the end of the day, you cannot make anyone do anything—they have to want it. By that time, you may have evolved into another woman, and you are no longer mentally present for them.

I believe that women leave mentally and emotionally before they leave physically.

One of the unspoken contributors that rarely gets named, yet profoundly shapes how we love, settle, and abandon ourselves, is nurtured neglect. What is that, you might ask? By nature, our design is to nurture. We are meant to care for and support others, encouraging the development of various aspects of life, be it children, someone's dreams, a business, or relationships—the list is endless.

If we are not careful, we can nurture our own neglect. Because Black women are conditioned to settle for less, this becomes a learned behavior—nurturing the very things that have harmed us.

When you grow up not receiving enough, you often learn to go without or to make do with what you have. This is similar to how you cope when you don't receive enough emotional sustenance. You were underfed emotionally, leading you to learn how to manage without it. What does that look like? It looks like being cared for physically but ignored emotionally.

Honestly, we both know that was the norm. It wasn't until recent years that Black people even began to consider emotions. In fact, it was often dismissed with remarks like, "Oh, you're depressed? Go wash those dishes," or "You haven't lived long enough to be depressed," or "You haven't been through anything to be sad all day."

This type of behavior isn't forgotten; it's absorbed. Now you may find yourself, consciously or unconsciously, telling yourself things like, "It's not that hard. I've had worse." Even if that statement is true, it conditions you to accept struggle as a prerequisite for living. Unconsciously, we echo sentiments from that quiet part of our mind: "But did you die?"

This is the beginning of nurturing neglect. What else could you do? As a Black woman, giving up wasn't an option. So you did what you knew best—adapt, survive, and evolve.

Let's discuss how this nurturing neglect actively validates abandonment wounds through actions and behaviors in real time. It longs for reciprocity—but it never arrives, so you adapt and adjust. It involves feeling and coming to terms with the reality that no one truly knows you, and that parts of you remain hidden because being vulnerable feels unsafe.

Nurturing neglect is being okay with being needed instead of being known.

This is nurturing neglect—accepting breadcrumbs because you don't believe you can have or attain something better. It's mistaking someone's effort for intimacy. It's believing that if you love him enough and give enough, he will magically become the man you need.

If I could just get him to the altar, that would be enough for me.

Nurturing neglect involves attracting and choosing partners who are projects rather than true partners. It's seeking partnership instead of purpose.

So what does it look like from your own perspective, you ask? Well, it can manifest as shutting down or minimizing your own need for space out of fear of being told you're too dramatic or to toughen up—or worse, hearing, "It's not that serious." I am sure someone will read this book and say aloud or to themselves that it's not that serious.

However, this is the reality for many Black women in America.

Again—another example of how we are expected to simply be okay when we go through experiences that affect our lives.

Returning to the topic.

Nurturing neglect can look like masking—telling people you're okay while hiding behind a facade, crying and wishing someone would hear or feel your pain. It involves offering advice or solutions while ignoring your own needs. It's changing the subject when things get deep because you won't allow yourself to feel.

You are nurturing neglect, ma'am!

You do all the emotional labor—planning, problem-solving, checking in—because you take pride in being the one who loves the unlovable and sticks it out. When you minimize the situation or rationalize the harm, you are nurturing neglect.

For instance, you might make excuses for him for not being consistent or emotionally present. You tell yourself, "At least he's still here; he comes home to me"—and that is enough, because you figure as long as the other woman doesn't have him, you are okay with that.

You dismiss and delay your own needs—and sometimes you do it before they can. You convince yourself that if you don't have any needs, then they can't disappoint you or hurt you.

So you won't need anything. You won't take up space. You won't get hurt. You prioritize everyone else's chaos and say things like, "I'll get to me later."

I heard on Instagram that "Priorities are just organized choices!" That shook me—because at the end of the day, it's all about choices and decisions. And I guess I wasn't important enough for you to choose me?

For my church girls—yes, let's bring it home.

For you, this may look like saying things like, "God is teaching me patience," when in reality, you are depriving yourself of intimacy and connection. Not because it's not available—but because you fear it. You fear it's too good to be true, so you live in a fantasy world of longing and waiting. But this is a mask to avoid change, to evade accountability for your actions, and to remain in perpetual cycles—which is akin to "faith without works is dead."

You cling to "God is going to send me my king" like it's a mantra—while refusing to learn the lessons from your actions. It's interpreting neglect as a test of your endurance, faith, or loyalty.

Based on everything I mentioned earlier, you should have an idea of your cycles and patterns. However, if you still believe in the existence of a perfect partner and that you can create one, then all of this was for nothing. There is no perfect partner, sis, and there is no knight in shining armor who will save you from all your troubles. Life will continue to unfold, and most of the time, it's about learning how to come together to overcome obstacles that deepen love and bond.

If you think this is going to be perfect, you will always be on the hunt—or, if you're an avoider, on the run. If you believe things aren't working because you're not doing enough and need to fix or change more, then the cycle will persist. It will continue until you understand that, at the end of the day, it's about what you are willing to love someone through—and them loving you through.

I am not saying to stay with someone who is abusive or hurts you. But I am saying that perfection is not real. There will always be something, and at this point in your life, you must choose from a place of safety—not lack or fear—and from a place of maturity.

What matters to you? What are your needs? What are your non-negotiables?

This is what's important. Because of trauma and abandonment wounds, you might not realize that there are core fundamental needs in a relationship. These needs support connection, healing, and mutual growth. When consistently met, they nurture security and self-worth. When absent, they create confusion, wounds, or survival patterns.

To give you an idea, let's discuss some basic needs in relationships, grouped by emotional, psychological, physical, and spiritual dimensions:

1. Emotional Needs

These create safety, vulnerability, and intimacy:

- Affection – Expressions of love and care through words, touch, and gestures
- Validation – Being seen, heard, and understood without judgment
- Empathy – Someone who can sit with your pain without trying to fix or minimize it
- Reassurance – Knowing you are wanted, safe, and emotionally secure
- Emotional Availability – Consistent presence, not just when it's convenient

2. Psychological Needs

These sustain identity, trust, and autonomy:

- Respect – Honoring each other's values, voice, boundaries, and experiences
- Honesty – Truthfulness in communication, even when it's hard
- Trust – Reliability, consistency, and confidentiality

- Freedom to Be Authentic – Space to show up fully without fear of punishment or rejection
- Mutual Accountability – Owning actions and repairing harm when needed

3. Relational/Social Needs

These reflect partnership and mutual support:

- Support – A partner in goals, healing, and everyday life
- Reciprocity – A balanced give and take, avoiding chronic overgiving or one-sidedness
- Shared Joy – Laughter, play, and meaningful time together
- Loyalty – Knowing someone has your back emotionally and relationally
- Conflict Resolution – The ability to work through differences with grace and maturity

4. Physical and Safety Needs

Even non-romantic relationships benefit from physical presence and safety:

- Physical Comfort – Non-sexual touch, body language, proximity (when welcome)
- Safety – Freedom from emotional, physical, or verbal harm
- Consistency – Reliability in action, words, and follow-through

5. Spiritual and Purpose-Oriented Needs

Especially in faith-based relationships, these elements deepen purpose and alignment:

- Shared Values or Beliefs – Not necessarily identical, but respectful of each other's faith journeys.
- Encouragement Toward Purpose – A partner who inspires you to reach your potential without shaming you.
- Spiritual Intimacy – Engaging in prayer together, speaking life into each other, or growing in alignment with your sacred callings.
- Grace and Forgiveness – The ability to love without expecting perfection and to repair without punishment.

Now that we've identified your needs, it's time to reflect on what you have accepted in the past. Before we can build something new, we must gently assess the patterns, people, and pain that have shaped how we love and how we allow ourselves to be loved. This is not about judgment; it's about truth. Truth is what sets us free.

I invite you to engage in this work—yes, in real time—to gain a deeper understanding of yourself. Let's get started.

The first step is awareness. What are the patterns you've noticed? What type of partners have you consistently been drawn to? What emotional, mental, physical, spiritual, or financial needs have you attempted to fulfill through these connections?

Remember: when you operate from a place of lack, your actions differ from when you come from a place of abundance. You have the opportunity to choose based on curiosity, growth, and other mature motivations, rather than out of lack and scarcity—such as needing to pay a bill, feeling lonely, or simply wanting someone to talk to.

Next, evaluate the cost. What did it cost you to be with this person? Did it take a toll on your time, energy, or finances? What relationships did you damage or neglect just to be with them? Did you sacrifice your voice or feel the need to shrink yourself to maintain the relationship?

Be vigilant about recognizing repetition in your experiences. Are there recurring dynamics or behaviors—such as emotional unavailability, ghosting, or over-functioning? This could apply to both you and your partner. Are you dating the same type of person but in a different context or location? It's concerning to realize that you might escape one toxic relationship only to find yourself in another similar situation. It may feel like your unresolved trauma and abandonment wounds are following you.

Now, confront your motivations. What compelled you to choose and stay with this person? What beliefs about yourself and the situation kept you from leaving?

The next step is action. It involves identifying the shifts and changes needed to reclaim your power and identity. Ask yourself, what do I need to do differently now? What relationship pattern am I ready to release?

You must be honest with yourself. You cannot continue with the mindset that things will simply get better if you just hold on. This requires a conscious effort; it's about being present in real-time—when something occurs, pause, pay attention, and try a different response than your usual one.

What if I said no to them—what would happen?

Before you know it, you'll find yourself taking actions and saying things that are best for you. You may look back and wonder, Did I really say that? Did I do that?

Before seeking something new, you must be honest about what you've allowed to persist in your life. You cannot build secure love on a foundation of survival.

Station 6

Give Him a Sound

Stuffed With Pain: When You Give Him a Voice That Mirrors Your Abandonment

In this station, we give voice to the silent ache that abandonment leaves behind. Rejection and ghosting don't just sting, they echo. For those carrying unhealed abandonment wounds, these experiences are more than disappointing; they feel like confirmation of an internal lie: I'm not wanted. I'm too much. I'll always be left.

When you've been conditioned to expect loss, even silence speaks loudly. And often, the sound you give your "bae" is the very voice of your own wounded inner child, begging not to be left behind again.

This chapter helps you name how abandonment disguises itself in dating dynamics, and how to begin reclaiming your voice from the patterns that have kept you chasing proof of your worth.

* * *

For someone with abandonment wounds, rejection and ghosting feel like an incessant sting. It doesn't merely suggest that a relationship didn't work out; it reinforces a belief that nobody wants them, providing proof of their worst fears. It serves as real-time evidence that they are too much or that people inevitably leave. This confirmation sinks in deeply, like a dog clinging to a bone.

Let's face it—no one enjoys being rejected. However, for someone suffering from abandonment wounds, the impact is even more profound. They internalize this pain, using it to berate themselves during difficult days. Whether someone stops responding after a meaningful conversation, disappears after sharing their best self, or engages in other forms of disconnection, the pain is intensified. It deepens the wounds and core beliefs stemming from childhood trauma, reinforcing the notion that love isn't safe and that people are unreliable.

The sudden and unexplained disappearance of someone can frustrate anyone, but for those with abandonment wounds and low self-worth, it becomes a mental battleground. They may spiral into sadness and darkness, from which it can take weeks or months to recover. This experience can lead to depression and other mental health issues, making individuals feel powerless and validating all the feelings of being unseen, unheard, unvalued, and unwanted.

Due to their abandonment wounds, they may have a history of being ghosted and rejected, but there is only so much one can endure. Ghosting is like the silent treatment on steroids; it leaves individuals in a state of confusion and vulnerability. It does not provide the closure they need and can trap them in a cycle of trying to understand what went wrong. It creates an empty void—silence where there should be connection.

This can also cause more damage to someone who has experienced abandonment. It can lead to increased trauma, prompting the person to withdraw and completely alter their outlook on life. It feels like punishment for trying, needing, and desiring connection. Instead of grieving the loss of that connection, she begins to mourn her own identity—a process that signifies a loss of self.

Unhealed rejection often results in lower self-worth, leading to settling for less than one deserves. Desperation sets in, and individuals may overcompensate in future relationships. Before long, they find themselves chasing after what they lost, trying to fill the void. This can result in becoming a serial dater, engaging in rebound relationships without any real intentions—simply to avoid being alone.

There are various forms of ghosting, the first of which is emotional. The absence of intimacy often triggers anxious attachment, making insecurities feel valid and prolonging the healing process.

It's important to acknowledge some truths: People often ghost or reject others for one of two reasons. First, they may recognize the work that needs to be done within you and feel unable to support you, which is their right and choice, as it's essential for them to love themselves and protect their peace. Second, they may lack the capacity to maintain the connection or grow alongside you.

When a woman with abandonment trauma is ghosted or rejected, it taps into her learned behaviors and reinforces negative beliefs. It connects to the part of her that believes no one sees her, no one cares, and that she is alone—ultimately leading to the belief that she will always be alone. This shifts her narrative toward settling for nothing, denying her heart's needs and desires for connection.

To cope with rejection and ghosting, she tells herself lies to justify moving forward. She avoids accountability for her actions and pushes through, and when she grows weary of being alone, she returns to the dating scene without making any changes. In the end, this cycle means nothing truly changes.

Often, it awakens the fixer within: Was I too much? What do I need to do to fix this or be better? How much weight do I need to lose to be more attractive—so I can impress others and avoid rejection in the future?

This is often where the villain in a woman's story begins—where she becomes the type who doesn't care, hurts others because she has been hurt, and dates to reclaim what she lost in a previous relationship, whether it was one that broke her heart or confirmed her fears of abandonment.

Rejection can also trigger a scarcity mindset: If this one said no, who else is left? I live in Atlanta—there are so many women for every man, especially a Black man. Most Black men are imprisoned, many are married, some are part of the LGBTQ+ community, others are on the down-low, and many harbor disdain for women—so what am I left with? There's not enough to go around. If someone leaves, I may never find another chance.

Let's discuss how to move from emotional destabilization to being rooted and grounded.

The first step is recognition—awareness. Once you recognize your feelings, you can name them. When you name them, you gain clarity about what you're experiencing and how to address it.

For instance, think of going to the doctor when you're sick. Before your visit, you might manage your symptoms on your own, assuming it's just a common cold. You rest, take medication, and follow your usual routine. But this time, it's different—it's not improving. Your ear starts to hurt, and you have trouble hearing. Your throat is sore, making it hard to talk. Now it's time for antibiotics. When you go to the doctor, you discover it's a sinus infection. All along, you were treating what you thought was a cold, but it wasn't. In this case, not knowing what it is can hinder your recovery —but once you identify the issue, you can take the appropriate steps to rectify the situation.

Next, you detach from false responsibility. This involves stopping the blame you place on yourself and ceasing the search for what you did wrong. Instead, focus on finding closure and extending compassion to yourself. Speak to the little girl inside you. Begin to self-soothe and sit with your feelings. Ask yourself questions to understand your emotions better. This process gives voice to your pain, prevents you from repeating patterns of avoidance, and sets you on the path to healing. It allows you to shift from reaction to redirection, reminding you of who you are and helping you reframe your experiences.

You work on setting boundaries and standards to elevate your life. Focus on improving your self-esteem and self-worth. Consider therapy to address the issues that brought you to this point, or commit to your mental, emotional, and spiritual care. You realign, reframe, and create affirmations from your pain by reclaiming your power—saying things like, "What's meant for me will never leave me, because what's for me is uniquely mine. I don't need to do anything to earn it, and there's nothing I can do to prevent it. It's for me."

Bring core beliefs—and at this moment, the lies—to the surface. Ask yourself: Is this true, or is this what I want to believe because it's easier? These are not just thoughts; they are survival statements you tell yourself to remain in perpetual cycles. You learned to believe that love, safety, and belonging must be earned through perfection, sacrifice, or over-functioning, making it difficult to discern the difference between self-worth and performance. Many of us were taught that love equals productivity, so shifting to a recognition of your worth will be challenging. After all, "all my life I had to fight!" (Color Purple reference).

Now, be mindful of the language you use—what you say becomes your reality. Pay attention to how you seek praise for your actions or believe you will be rewarded with marriage for how long and hard you've supported someone. This mindset teaches you that your worth is conditional and that you are only as valuable as your next achievement.

Self-worth, independent of performance, means that you are more than just what you can achieve. It signifies that you are worthy of love simply for being who you are.

Let's address the challenging question: Who are you when you are not performing? It's a good question, isn't it? And you may not have an answer, because throughout your life, you've had to fight. This requires strength and courage. It compels you to sit with yourself and learn who you truly are—either from the beginning or all over again. Who are you when you are not needed? Do you even like yourself? What about your body? Do you embrace that stomach? Learning to love yourself without doing anything, without trying to fix things—or even trying to fix you—is essential.

To avoid bitterness, you must establish boundaries and understand what emotional resilience looks like. Emotional resilience is the ability to prevent trauma, setbacks, or crises from overwhelming you—to be able to bounce back. How do you avoid becoming bitter and rigid? You learn where your feelings are coming from. Are they stemming from an unhealed place or a healed one?

To determine this, you need to listen and observe. What are you saying, and how are you saying it? The body may lie, and the mouth may deceive, but the heart will reveal the truth. Often, it has no filter.

Now, let's examine your behavior. What's your motivation? Are you striving to impress others, or are you acting out of self-love and a desire for your own well-being? Are you honoring your emotions, providing them a safe space to be felt and heard, or are you suppressing them and moving on to the next thing? Are you shutting down and throwing a temper tantrum, or are you giving your feelings a voice, no longer hiding behind avoidance and the wounded inner child?

Learning to move, respond, and choose from a place of healing —rather than from your history—is a sign that you are cultivating emotional resilience. You are no longer allowing ghosting and rejection to define you; instead, you let them redirect you. This shift enables you to make better choices—saying no sooner and walking away faster from things that don't serve you, without feeling guilty, regretting your decision, or fearing that you may not get another opportunity like that again.

Sidenote: In fact, you're right—you don't want another chance like that again.

From the previous chapter, you learned the difference between being cherished and being chosen. As you continue on this growth journey, you begin to see all relationships as opportunities for growth and evolution. Just because you are not dating does not mean you are healed; it simply indicates that no one is triggering your abandonment wound, allowing it to remain dormant—until fear about time or other factors sets in.

Remember, it's not a destination—it's a return. A return to home, to yourself, and to who you were meant to be.

You can work on yourself and still be worthy. You don't have to wait until you are "fully healed," because what does that really look like? Once you understand that none of us are perfect—and that we must love someone through their challenges—you can choose what you want to love someone through, and how you want to do it. Ultimately, it should not come at the expense of your well-being.

It is essential to understand and be aware of your behaviors. Next, you must have the courage to confront yourself and challenge these behaviors. Recognize that you are not just dating the same type of person, but rather, you are dating your patterns.

I heard a relationship and dating coach named Anwar White on a YouTube podcast called Awf The Record state that our type is really our trauma. As we emerge from survival mode and heal our trauma, we realize that what once nourished us no longer does— and that our type often reflects unhealed trauma.

What do those patterns look like? They include over-giving, rescuing, proving, staying too long, people-pleasing, and fixing. To break the cycle and start anew, you must detach from these behaviors. This is why letting go is so challenging; these patterns have become part of your identity.

Starting over—yes, at this stage in your life—requires confronting the reality that you've been wrong all along, which involves admitting failure. Remaining attached to these patterns means that, with awareness, you are choosing to stay this way and avoid the hard work because it feels uncomfortable. You may believe that releasing these patterns equates to giving up, and the thought of losing everything you've invested in them can be even more painful. So, where do you go from here? How do you move on?

You begin by learning to make choices based on self-worth rather than emotional hunger. Remember, we discussed earlier that scarcity can drive us to make irrational decisions.

Station 7

Host the Ceremony

Before You Box Him Up and Take Him Home, Crown Yourself

This station marks a sacred pause a moment to reflect before you take home what you've built. For so long, Black women have been praised for their endurance but rarely celebrated for their boundaries. We've been taught that love means labor, that staying means strength, and that worth is earned through sacrifice.

But before you box him up and carry him into your life, it's time to ask: Have I crowned myself first?

This chapter invites you to honor the generations who carried, while giving yourself permission to choose differently. You're not abandoning legacy—you're expanding it. The ceremony isn't for him, it's for you.

* * *

From a young age, Black women are often taught, either directly or indirectly, that love is something to be held onto tightly, something to endure, and that one's worth is tied to what one can do and give. We have been culturally conditioned to carry the load. Phrases like "Ride or Die" reinforce this notion, praising those who are resilient while ridiculing those who prioritize their own well-being. Throughout history, our mothers, grandmothers, and ancestors have borne these burdens, passing the mantle from generation to generation. I won't blame them, but I will challenge them to create space for change. Given the shifts in society, we as women today have the opportunity to redefine our roles.

I remember when I was young—around 13 years old but feeling much older due to the hardships I faced. If you know, you know: trauma and hardship can make you mature before your time. My great-grandmother, my grandmother's mother, was in a nursing home bed. She used to be a fireball, often saying things that made you wish you had just sent a gift instead of visiting her. But after sending that gift, you'd feel it was better to see her in person.

I recall a time when she asked me how old I was and insisted it was time for me to start a family—meaning get married and have kids. I looked at her, wide-eyed and shocked, and jokingly replied that this wasn't *The Color Purple*, Big Momma. Kids don't have kids anymore, and that's not how things work these days. She looked shocked but remained firm in her stance.

Later in life, I began to be picked on and ridiculed for not having a boyfriend, stable relationships, and eventually for not being married. Meanwhile, my family was getting married left and right, often to the same people over and over again. One day, I reached my breaking point and decided to give them a taste of what they were giving me. Unfortunately, my response came out bitter, angry, and sad. I became the loud Nay-Nay, a persona that is still hard to shake off. Eventually, I stopped trying to change it because I realized we all have parts of ourselves that others cling to, and I told myself to let them. After all, I had tried to rectify my bad behaviors, but there's only so much one can do.

It wasn't until I got older that I understood why my grandmother frequently mentioned the importance of having a husband. It seemed that, in her eyes, one wasn't truly seen or valued until they were married. This marked the beginning of my healing process, where I learned to stop viewing everything as an attack and instead see it from a place of love. I knew my family loved me, but it was hard to accept. So, I decided to pick myself up and focus on self-improvement. That's when it dawned on me: what if my family, especially my grandmother, was expressing concern out of worry and fear? In her time, having a husband meant provision and protection. Could she have been worried about my future and concerned that I wouldn't be okay? Was she advising me to pursue these things to ensure I wouldn't be left without support?

I then changed how I perceived the verbal taunting and chose to see it as a reflection of their concern for me. Statistically, Black women today are the most educated and earn the most money. So, while my family witnessed my success and my ability to support myself—accomplishments that they couldn't achieve in their time— it didn't seem to matter to them. In their minds, without a husband, I was still considered lower than a second-class citizen.

I took it upon myself to educate them and let them know that I am fine on my own—that I don't need a husband for security, provision, or other support—and that times have changed. However, because my family is close-knit, those ideas often get dismissed. I enjoy my time with them and gently make jokes about their lives. After all, nobody wants to be called out for their past mistakes or behaviors; it's about mutual respect.

Because of this mindset, many Black women have endured significant hardships and negative behaviors from their husbands. They have faced cheating, discovering another family, being ghosted, abandoned, and left to raise children while struggling to make ends meet. Additionally, many have faced rejection due to their skin color. While I don't want to delve too deeply into colorism, it is a real issue. Within our community, those with darker skin are often treated as secondary, while women with lighter skin are often chosen. That said, women with lighter complexions also face their own struggles, though I can't speak to those experiences.

I've heard that being considered "too pretty" can come with its own challenges, as it may attract attention that can lead to envy and harm. Unfortunately, this continues to happen today, but I hope this book not only raises awareness of these issues but also unites us to foster change.

Let's be honest—Black women are healing from survival mode, trauma, and unmet emotional needs, and battling these challenges without an outlet can lead to toxicity. These issues manifest in relationships in various ways; for example, the hypervigilant "high-functioning Black girl magic" woman may find herself anxious and on high alert for signs of ghosting or disapproval. This mindset influences our decision-making, driving us to people-please to avoid loneliness and to prove others wrong, often attracting unavailable partners due to unhealed wounds.

Much of this has been discussed in previous chapters, but let's explore how rejection, abandonment, and cultural expectations shape the way women love in relationships. It begins with a system: in white settings, you must be perfect; in Black family environments, you must be quiet and obedient; in church, you must be holy; and in relationships, you must be everything. A saying used to keep us in line was, "What you won't do, Susie up the street will." This instills a fear of abandonment, leading us to take desperate measures to avoid being left behind.

How does this manifest in us? It often appears as shrinking and biting your tongue to avoid being seen as combative—fearing the labels of "angry Black woman," "too much," "too emotional," or "dramatic." It looks like minimizing yourself to maintain peace and make your partner feel secure, even when you know you are right—truly right. It means settling for less and tolerating behavior that shouldn't be acceptable, believing it's better to have him around than to be alone, all while thinking you need to be a good little girl earning love that should be freely given.

The absence of fathers—due to incarceration, addiction, or death—forces women into dual roles, adopting both feminine and masculine traits out of necessity, not choice. The show must go on. Can you imagine being raised by a mother who is doing everything she can to care for her children, self-sacrificing and neglecting her own needs? Well, yeah. The apple doesn't fall far from the tree.

Add your upbringing to a mother who is emotionally distant, always working, and not truly present when she is home; all of this has shaped the woman you are today. Culturally, the interplay of nature versus nurture, attachment theory, and trauma has placed you in survival mode, just like your mom, teaching you the beliefs you hold today. These factors influence how you love, as you learned to do so by observing your mother, and they contribute to the woman you are because you have not yet broken the cycle to bring about change.

These internalized roles—rooted in history, culture, faith, and trauma—teach Black women to love through sacrifice rather than safety.

How this is formed or what it looks like:

- *Generational messages:* Don't cry—it's a sign of weakness. Be grateful because we had less. Be strong—you're the oldest. Take care of others—it's the right thing to do.

- *Church messages:* Endure like Ruth. Suffer like Job. Serve like Martha.

- *Societal messages:* Black women can do anything—they are strong; however, they are often seen as unlovable and intolerable.

This mindset manifests as "As long as my kids are okay, I am okay." It reflects being raised to keep the family together, bearing the burden of responsibility like Big Momma—because if you don't, the family may fall apart. You grew up being a second mother, even when it wasn't explicitly asked of you, simply because your mom worked all the time. You learned to be useful to avoid being over-looked or forgotten.

These experiences taught you about love: that love often meant neglecting your own needs, leading to a loss of self. Your pain felt unimportant, as if you were asked, "But did you die?" Mental, emotional, physical, and spiritual exhaustion became expected and normalized. In fact, were you truly doing anything if you weren't giving your all or self-sacrificing? Can you even consider it a genuine effort?

What are the results of this mindset and upbringing? They often lead to attracting partners who take without giving. This creates an inability to ask for what she needs due to feelings of guilt and fear about taking up space. As a result, she criticizes herself for taking breaks or resting, which are often viewed as selfish. Some people may even make her feel self-centered for prioritizing her own needs. She feels guilty for being sick because it prevents her from being productive. If she cannot accomplish tasks, she wonders who can or will.

This ties back to the earlier discussed mindset: I am only lovable if I am needed.

A related cultural aspect within some church communities is the belief that if she serves harder, attends every meeting, and gives everything she has, then God will view her as worthy and send her a partner. This mindset suggests that devotion to the church will make her a worthy candidate for love, reinforcing the idea that church rewards performance and operates under law rather than grace. The belief is that if she does good, she will be rewarded; conversely, if she is not rewarded, it must mean she is not doing enough. This leads to a focus on submission over discernment, viewing love as a reward for sacrifice—even though Jesus has already paid it all.

Consequently, she becomes a "Holy Hustler," believing that while her life and body are sacred, her heart and emotions are not. This mindset causes her to remain in unhealthy situations, thinking she must be faithful. She spiritualizes her struggles, believing she must suffer her way into a blessing, which ultimately results in emotional neglect.

Let's discuss the dismissed daughter, for whom nothing she does is ever enough. The sons are glorified and treated well, given chances and opportunities to learn and make mistakes, while she is ridiculed and scorned for having the audacity to feel. She grew up in the shadows, often overlooked and becoming the scapegoat for issues within the home. She learns that rejection and loneliness are expected and doesn't seek anything different, fearing the repercussions of doing so. She overgives, over-apologizes, and stays just to avoid being alone. She chases affection through her actions and accepts abandonment as its reward.

I provided these examples to lay the groundwork for understanding how the girl became the fixer and the builder. The ingredients of her life expose the lie and illuminate her story, undoing the misconception about love—that one must survive hardship to earn it, and that love is a paycheck for all the times one had to clock in for work.

Love is a birthright, sister, and you don't have to endure pain to be rewarded for it. Yes, there will be ups and downs; that comes with everything in life—but the lie that "love is pain" is untrue. Love is patient. Love is kind. Love always seeks to protect. Love perseveres. And love never fails.

I am sure we can all relate to the various roles presented earlier —whether you are the church girl, a family caretaker, the dismissed daughter, or, like me, the high-functioning daughter. These roles can cause us to stay too long, leading to burnout and sometimes resulting in poor decisions that hurt ourselves and others.

If you ever find yourself in such a place in your life, don't be ashamed! Ask for help. Seek your nearest hospital and get the support you need. You can text or call the suicide hotline at 988 for assistance.

Next, let's address the secret belief that suffering equals loyalty. We were taught that to truly be committed, you must endure hardship. One must be cautious when dating because there are men who say things like, "I want a woman like my mother." What they really mean is that they witnessed their mother endure challenges alone, managing everything and still pushing through. They want that same resilience in you. Most of the time, this comes from good intentions, but it perpetuates a harmful cycle.

I am quite sure that if his father had been present, his mother wouldn't have had to shoulder so much of the burden. It's important to recognize that relationships are meant to be partnerships where help is shared, not one person carrying the entire load. Yes, we can do everything, but we weren't created to bear such weight alone.

I know I might be catching some side-eyes from you wonderfully independent sisters—and that's okay. You have every right to be everything you aspire to be. My goal here is to remind you that your worth is not defined by how much you endure or suffer.

If you want to work hard, pursue a higher position, and chase your dreams, that's admirable—I applaud you. I stand beside you with my own ambitions. However, the aim of this book is to empha-size that soft, safe, and gentle love is available—and if you desire it, you must choose better.

I once had a man tell me about dating: "There is nothing wrong with you—you just need to pick better. The guys you choose aren't really men, and when a real man comes along, it scares you, and you don't know how to respond." I asked him what I was doing that gave off that impression, and I'm grateful he helped me recognize the behaviors I exhibited that suggested I wasn't fully healed. I knew that, but I was surprised he could see it in less than three months.

It was the way I spoke that made the difference. I sounded as though I was asking and begging for things, while a man who was walking in abundance—healed and confident—would give freely.

Let's explore the origins of the belief that suffering equals loyalty. This belief didn't begin with you, of course. It stemmed from observation and experience: witnessing your mother endure a loveless marriage for the sake of the children, seeing a grandmother pray through decades of neglect, and growing up in a culture that equated exhaustion with strength while overlooking hidden emotional wounds.

It's important to recognize that some of this is our own doing. For instance, we often mask and hide our true feelings well. We've been part of a church that glorified long-suffering and labeled boundaries and standards as rebellion or Jezebel.

When loyalty comes at the cost of betraying yourself, the price is too high!

Let's clarify this: suffering is not proof of faith, as some might believe. Suffering is not a love language, and putting someone through hardship to prove their commitment is not a love language either. Suffering should not be equated with commitment.

Remaining loyal to pain, suffering, and struggle is not love—it's toxic and detrimental to self-esteem.

Let's discuss the misuse of submission, forgiveness, and waiting, which keeps women trapped in cycles of emotional abandonment. Believe it or not, this is a spiritual weapon used to prevent women from realizing their full potential—both inside and outside the church. It's a tactic to keep your heart broken, robbing you of hope, belief, and faith.

This becomes abuse when misunderstood obedience is disguised as submission. We must remember what we were taught—that suffering is love, and to maintain a relationship, self-sacrifice is necessary, often masquerading as quiet submission. To honor your husband, you must be seen and not heard, sacrificing your needs for the greater good, rather than ensuring both parties work together for the well-being of the relationship.

You were taught that forgiveness meant letting someone back in —not realizing that nothing has changed. When you forgive and let them back in, you lose pieces of yourself. As a result, your wounds remain unhealed and unnoticed, causing your self-esteem to plummet. The emotional wounds begin to fester, creating more hurtful core beliefs and narratives.

In the church, women are praised for waiting on the Lord; if they don't, they are scolded and ridiculed. Often, they feel embarrassed for desiring a mate, rather than being supported in pursuing what could be a positive next chapter in their lives. Preparing for marriage—seeking counsel, taking courses, and reading books on how to be a good wife—is viewed with disdain.

People may say things like, "That's putting the cart before the horse," suggesting you are worried about the wrong things. However, I believe this mindset contributes to the high divorce rates within the church. There is an expectation to endure—like with everything else—and simply trust in the Lord instead of prioritizing healing and personal growth beforehand.

This leads women to spiritualize their waiting, causing them to remain in unfulfilling situations, cling to false hope, and ignore red flags in the name of faith. Rather than being encouraged that pursuing personal development is valuable, they are dismissed because it is seen as a man's responsibility to find a wife, and any initiative on their part is discouraged.

On the other hand, there is a contradictory expectation. If a woman is fulfilled, has done the necessary work, and is advancing in her career without prioritizing marriage, she may be persecuted for being too independent. It seems that her entire existence is expected to revolve around finding a husband and submitting her life to him. Despite her fulfillment, others may imply that she hasn't done enough or suffered enough, making her feel guilty for choosing herself and pursuing whatever relationship makes her happy.

Sis, you are allowed to want soft love! I remember a conversation I had with my mother about how my boyfriend at the time was treating me, and I didn't understand why. I told her that when I was on my cycle, he babied me—he was kinder and nicer to me. We both concluded that this was because I needed him; I was down and out, unable to do anything but breathe, let alone make something to eat or drink. He would ask me if I was hungry, and sometimes I would just curl up and cry, "Yes."

I could not be that strong Black woman all the time—I had to sit down and just be a woman. He was able to shine, and I said out loud, "How do I get that all the time? What am I doing that gives off 'I got it' vibes? Because a girl is tired." I then expressed, not fully realizing it, that I wanted someone to take care of me. My mom responded, "Not me, not my daughter. My daughter can take care of herself." I raised my voice, saying, "No, I am tired! I know I can, but I want to be taken care of."

That was when I realized that wanting soft love was a solo journey, and I needed to stop discussing all my personal relationships with my mom because we didn't want the same things. There was a moment when she told my dad not to help me with something that

needed to go into my car because I could do it. I replied, "Yes, I
could, but if Dad wants to do it, I'm going to let him." I thought to
myself, you are always fussing at me to let a man be a man, and this
was me doing just that.

I learned again that my story and the things I desired would
never come to fruition if I continued to listen to those who neither
wanted it nor could envision it for me. This is not an attack on my
mom, but rather a realization that, in order to reach my goal of
allowing myself to receive gentle love, I had to stop heeding the
advice of those who were content with harsh love. We were not the
same.

I often felt anger and frustration toward my mom because she
would say things like, "Oh, you guys could have worked it out," or
"You should have stayed," or "Give it more time." While I have
come to recognize that she was right about some things over the
years, I eventually started to think, "This lady doesn't like me..." I
said to myself, "She loves me, but she doesn't like me. Why would
she tell me to stay with someone who ghosted me every two weeks?"
I confronted her, saying, "Mom, this man has another family!"

If there was one relationship that taught me what is meant for
me is for me, it was that one. The way he would come and go from
my life was embarrassing. I remember wailing and crying so
intensely that my daughter came into the room to check on me. I
had never cried in front of her before and was spiraling like never
before. I asked her, "What did I do wrong? Why is he online but not
answering me?" She then took my phone from me because I
couldn't stop trying to call him, desperate to understand what I had
done wrong so I could fix it.

I was lost. I even went to my parents' house and cried on their
couch. I felt so low that I was afraid to be alone, fearing I might do
something irrational. I drove by his job and called to see if he was
there. Ugh, God! I even had my cousin call his number to see if he
would answer her, but he didn't. I was lost, and once I emerged
from that darkness, I vowed never to return.

I also learned that although my mom was my pastor and a
prophet, she was not my God. I had to prioritize what was best for

me. That year, things changed, and I began to work diligently on my healing. I realized that my actions were affecting everything around me, including my daughter. Unconsciously, I was starting a new generation of unhealed abandonment wounds, as her father never took the time to build a relationship with her. Growing up with a single mother, I—unhealed and unaware—repeated the same pattern.

I decided to break that cycle in my relationships, especially since almost every member of my family has been married four times or has been separated for over ten years. I wanted more. There had to be more! When I saw on Instagram men washing their partners' hair, cooking for them, feeding them, and providing space for them to feel and think without having to sacrifice themselves—Black men, no less!—I thought, "There's no way I'm going back."

Begging someone for the decency of reciprocity and consistency was exhausting. But believing it for myself was the real challenge. No more cooking, cleaning, and being intimate just to prove I would make a good wife. No more staying longer in church, working harder, or praying louder for God to notice me as a good little soldier. No more holding pain for others before learning to tend to my own needs. No more being a ride-or-die in hopes of being noticed! No more equating performance or productivity with love!

I refused to date emotionally unavailable men who neglected and protected me. I am free! I wanted soft love—the love that was inherently mine, because it's my birthright! No more standing for systems that abandon me just to go with the flow. No more protecting the relationships of those who taught me that I must be deemed worthy to be cherished—or that lighter skin, beautiful hair, and a skinny body are the only paths to love.

From now on, it will be safe love—love that is mutual, affirming, consistent, and peaceful. Love that stands firm and eliminates any signs of ambiguity. A love that doesn't fear discomfort out of concern for abandonment. It's a love that comes from within—a love I cultivate for myself. A love that sets the standards and is always accessible when I need it. It's safe. It's soft. It's vulnerable.

Yes, we were taught to be strong, but I am offering you a world of both softness and strength. This was not offered, modeled, and often punished. But now, I ask you to extend the same strength you gave to that man, the same understanding you offered that relation-ship—to yourself!

If you cry, it's no longer "Hush before I give you something to cry about." Instead, it's "What's wrong?" If you need help, there is no shame waiting for you on the other side. It's "What can I do for you? What do you need? How can I support you?" If you need rest, there's no guilt for being tired and exhausted. It's seen as recovery and part of your self-care.

No more performing, no more over-functioning, no more accepting breadcrumbs and calling it love or holding someone down. It's a place where you don't have to beg for clarity, affection, or consistency in a relationship—it's already given. In fact, it's the bare minimum. You deserve that. Being in a relationship with someone who is whole and healthy should come naturally.

I'm not saying people are perfect, but at this point in your life, you have the power to choose—and not let your fears choose for you.

Part Two

The Rebuild

Station 8

The Factory Reset

Rewiring the System: When Faith Formed You in Fear, Not Freedom

I n this station, we confront one of the most complex wounds: when faith intended to liberate has instead been used to confine. For many Black women, spiritual teachings have shaped not just beliefs, but their very blueprint for love, worth, and endurance. And too often, that shaping was rooted in fear, not freedom.

This chapter invites you to gently examine where your faith walk was filtered through guilt, performance, or punishment. Where you were taught to suffer quietly, serve endlessly, or shrink spiritually for the sake of being "chosen."

Here, we begin the reset not to abandon faith, but to reclaim it. Because love rooted in fear will always make you feel like you're not enough. But faith rooted in freedom reminds you: you already are.

* * *

I mention many church-related topics in this book because they are integral to African American culture. In one way or another, a Black woman's life has been shaped by religious or cultural beliefs. If this does not resonate, then this book may not be for her—but it's valuable to empathize with your closest sister.

Let's explore how this can become a weapon that often traps women in perpetual toxic cycles. For many, their suffering and stagnation are linked to spiritual discipline. They may think, "I must have done something wrong," or "I'm not doing enough or doing it right." This mindset leads to repeated cycles of feeling lost, inadequate, and lowering their standards just to have someone—or, at times, they may even give up altogether.

This phenomenon validates what they already believe deep down: that they are not good enough, that they weren't chosen for marriage, or that the people around them with loving and successful relationships somehow imply that they are meant to be the sacrificial figure in the group.

I want you to understand that there are seasons when having a husband and marriage is not the goal, sis. The aim of this book is to illustrate that waiting on God is entirely different from waiting for someone to choose you.

Waiting on God while trying to prove your worthiness—so He doesn't leave—is not the same as waiting on God while choosing yourself, doing the necessary work, and being able to make better choices. That's the path of healing, should you choose it.

Earlier in a previous chapter, I mentioned how church women often become enamored with the fantasy that God will send them a husband, but they lack the faith walk and accountability to make it happen. They hide behind a false mirage, thinking this illusion is sufficient—unaware that it is not real. I want to delve deeper into that topic.

Next, let's discuss the obedient woman, who often embodies obedience that masquerades as fear. It communicates a lack of trust in God; if she truly trusted Him, she would prepare and not harbor fear beneath the surface. Believe it or not, the pressures from the world, the church, and family significantly influence your decisions.

You say you are waiting on God, but you are endlessly dating.

You claim to be waiting on God, yet you don't even consider men who are committed to valuing their relationship with the Father.

You say you are waiting on God, but you keep lowering your standards.

It sounds to me like you don't truly believe. You seem tired of waiting and have decided to give God a hand, much like Sarah did. You think, "If I submit enough, sacrifice enough, and remain silent—because men prefer quiet women—maybe I can find one."

Well, sis, this is the recipe for losing yourself.

It suggests that you are tired and impatient.

Because of that, I had to learn the hard way.

The hard way, you ask?

Yes—let me tell you what that looked like.

It looked like me settling for a relationship where I tolerated bad treatment and often found myself dragged through the mud. And because it was a Christian relationship, I gave it more space in my life, thinking that by labeling it with God, everything would be alright.

I thought that as long as he was a Christian and actively serving in the church, I was doing well. I believed that if I labeled it a Christian relationship, surely this must be it.

Mannnn… that relationship took me through all kinds of turmoil—and you know why?

Because I wasn't meant to be in it.

I thought the hardships were just part of the relationship—the ups and downs. Never mind that he was triggering me, gaslighting me, and causing me significant emotional distress. At that time, I believed I had to suffer for love, and since it was a Godly love, I thought it was a spiritual warfare thing.

Yeah—it was. One that was sent by God to get me out of there! Haha!

Not the kind meant to test and teach you, but one meant to show me: leave that alone. God will handle it.

It brought to life the truth of the scripture:

"The blessing of the LORD, it maketh rich, and he addeth no sorrow with it." —Proverbs 10:22

I remember when one of my relationships went really bad, and I spiraled. During my healing process—taking time to recover from that relationship—I realized that I didn't date wisely; I dated out of fear. In that time of healing, I immersed myself in my faith, and God spoke to me as clearly as day. He said, "You can't just marry anyone."

At that time, I was bringing men to God as if I were searching for a lost puppy. I would ask, "Will this one work, God? Okay, how about this one? Will this one work? This one's in the church and does music and ministry—I know this one will work!"

Eventually, I came to see that the issue wasn't with them—it was with me. God was trying to show me that whenever I entered a relationship, I was self-sacrificing both myself and Him. I became so focused on not losing them and on being the best girlfriend or wife I could be that I neglected my own needs. I stopped pursuing my goals, ministry, and spiritual focus. I even stopped spending time with God because I was so caught up with the guy.

Then one day, God spoke to me, asking, "Am I not more than ten husbands?" (referencing what Elkanah said to his wife Hannah in 1 Samuel 1:8), and I broke down and cried. I repented, but it took time for me to change my behaviors. I had to dig deep and search for the root of the issue. Why was I prioritizing others over myself? Why was I giving up time, energy, and other irreplaceable things to keep someone who wasn't doing anything to earn it? It was just given.

It was because I wanted them more than I wanted myself!

At the time, I didn't recognize that this was rooted in low self-worth, though I did understand it stemmed from abandonment issues. However, I wasn't taking significant action. I was merely trying to change my behavior without addressing my beliefs. To have something meaningful and maintain it, I needed to believe it was meant for me. I had to change my inner self before I could see the manifestation of those changes on the outside.

I was more in love with the idea that God was going to send me my husband than I realized; if He did, I would have totally jacked him up! I didn't see that my hurt was spilling over into every aspect of my life. But I wasn't able to change—well, not in the moment. I was in survival mode, doing whatever I had to do just to get by.

I thought I was being Spirit-led, but in fact, I was complying based on trauma. I was obeying the God I had been taught about—one who instilled fear. "You go to hell for this. You go to hell for that."

So, it was only natural for me to fall into performance to please God, because that's what I had always done. I was good at it! Years passed, during which I ignored my needs, dedicating myself to spiritual work but not offering enough care for myself.

It wasn't until I broke and had enough—when I grew tired of God and the church and decided to just be—that freedom came. The pressures of performance decreased, allowing me to see my flaws and mistakes. I realized that I didn't really know Jesus as well as I thought, and that there was so much more to discover!

I learned that true relationship involves behavior, and that the holy work of being holy—dying to myself—was really about dismissing my own needs. I had been silencing my struggles, imagining them away simply by laying them at the altar. But in truth, those issues were waiting for me at home—in the silent, quiet space.

I told myself lies when I went to church, smiling at the sisters and participating in ministry. I convinced myself that it was okay to ignore what was in my heart and my desire for connection.

Eventually, I began to see that God created relationships to heal. However, because I was taught that desiring connection and intimacy was wrong, I remained in denial. I fought against it. In fact, I believe that this struggle is the reason some of us are still struggling today.

It's because you are in denial about your basic human need for connection. As a result, you neglect yourself and refrain from fulfilling that need. You might overwork, overcompensate in relationships, use sex as an outlet, binge eat, or turn to drugs.

When I realized that God cares about the whole person, not just the spiritual, I began to do the work. I'm trying to emphasize that there are LAYERS TO THIS! Growth is not just linear; it's non-linear. This perspective allows for improvement rather than perfection.

You start to understand that nurturing neglect manifests as thoughts like, "God will heal me in time," without any effort on your part. It can involve using prayer, giving it to Jesus, or laying it at the altar as a way to avoid the necessary process. You might be encouraged to pray about your struggles without ever being held accountable for your behavior.

Understand this: unprocessed wounds don't disappear in worship; they hide in obedience and performance.

I want to stay on this track of being married to the idea and fantasy. Even while you trust and wait for God to send you a husband, your actions may not reflect that belief. You might avoid intimacy out of fear of being hurt or feeling vulnerable. You may date emotionally unavailable men, deceived by their outward appearance as Christians, even though their actions do not align with their beliefs.

It's as if you prioritize Christianity over character. And believe it or not, this is a real issue.

Another form of conditioning—do you remember when I referenced the "Waiting to Exhale" meme, "He's a good man, Savannah"? This is similar! It's the pressure to be with someone simply because they are saved and "equally yoked," while ignoring the fact that this person is not emotionally, mentally, physically, or financially available or mature.

You are told to overlook these shortcomings because he attends church—that's considered the most important aspect. Not how he treats you. Not how he makes you feel. Just the fact that he goes to church.

One must be cautious about the unspoken cultural conditioning. At the end of the day, the church may avoid criticizing you, won't label you a Jezebel, and won't assume you're after their husband or pastor simply because you're single. They will make you feel that having any godly man is better than being alone.

In this area, it is safe to trust God and His plan for your life.

We often think that a lack of chemistry means God is saying no. In reality, it may simply be our nervous system feeling calm and untriggered, which we mistakenly interpret as a lack of love.

When a healed or healthy man comes along, we often don't make ourselves available. We dodge opportunities, leave church early, and feel conflicted.

We convince ourselves he's not the right man for us—he's not our type, he's lame, or he's unattractive.

Then, we find ourselves attracted to the type of person we initially rejected, and the cycle repeats.

You might feel that God shouldn't be in charge of your love life because you worry He will send you someone you don't find attractive or someone who won't bring you joy in the long run.

Let's be honest: many of us think that God will send us a man we wouldn't even want to be intimate with.

This belief can lead you to lower your standards in an attempt to "help God out."

You may dismiss red flags in a person, telling yourself, "No one's perfect," but we both know we only make exceptions for what we truly want. If he wasn't what you wanted or needed, you would have already let him go.

I believe people's tolerance for unacceptable behavior is much longer when they desire something.

I've seen women stay in marriages because they see it as a ministry.

Whether you believe in divorce or not, that isn't the biggest factor here. The root of the issue is often fear. You stay because you believe you are meant to endure this, and that belief is the core problem.

Then, the idea of divorce becomes another reason to keep you tethered to the marriage.

Sometimes, one may stay out of sheer embarrassment over a breakup—men often seem to move on easily, while women are bombarded from the pulpit with messages about submission and behavior, leading them to feel lucky just to have been in a relationship.

This creates a new behavior where obedience is mistaken for intimacy with God, but in truth, it is a suppression of self.

One way to determine if you are being ruled by fear and survival mode is to ask yourself, "What part of me feels unsafe with this choice—my spirit or my survival mode?" This question allows you to reflect and helps you step back from the situation.

When you are too close to something, you can become fixated on every minor detail and issue, leading you to react to each one. However, if you take a step back, you may realize, "That didn't require that much energy."

As you gain this perspective, you also begin to learn to trust God and understand His plan for your life.

Station 9

The Repair Station

Mending the Mess, Patching the Pain, Stitching the Seams, and Sewing Yourself Whole

This station is where the rebuilding begins not of another "bae," but of you. Healing abandonment isn't just about who left it's about who you became trying to survive it. Now, you're invited to return to yourself with softness, honesty, and care.

Here, we begin the slow, sacred work of self-repair. This is where you learn to reattach to your worth, reparent your inner child, and create safety from the inside out. It's not just about avoiding future heartbreak it's about mending what was never your fault and reclaiming what was always your birthright: wholeness.

This is the station of deep healing. And beloved, you deserve every stitch.

* * *

Let's discuss self-repair and reattachment. The next few chapters will focus on getting out of survival mode, healing abandonment wounds, reparenting the inner child, establishing boundaries, and fostering healing.

Healing abandonment wounds isn't just about preventing people from leaving you; it's about reattaching to your own wholeness. This beautiful journey involves listening to your inner voice and enhancing your self-worth. It is an invitation to healing, emotional sovereignty, and the opportunity to redefine what safety and love mean from the inside out.

Let's break this down. An internal split often occurs when one endures hardship and trauma. Individuals develop coping mechanisms to protect themselves, which can evolve into survival strategies. This may manifest as behaviors discussed in previous chapters—over-giving, perfectionism, and sometimes dissociation.

This split undermines our trust in ourselves. Due to patterns of self-sacrifice and self-abandonment, it can be challenging to set boundaries or commit to actions and follow through on them.

When those people left, you didn't just lose them; you lost parts of yourself by doing whatever it took to keep them in your life. You may find yourself secretly leaving parts of yourself open, hoping they will return. You linger in sadness, waiting for closure and understanding, unaware of how the pursuit of closure traps you in a cycle.

Waiting for closure is a time thief. It's akin to comparison—it can be destructive. Closure can hold you hostage, making you believe it is the key to your freedom. But it's not; it's a trap and a falsehood. You don't need closure—you desire it. You want it because you hope they will explain what went wrong so you can attempt to fix it. You seek validation for the narrative that something is wrong with you, reinforcing the lie that people always leave and no one ever stays. You date in an attempt to redeem the abandonment wound, rather than heal it.

What is self-repair, and what does it look like?

Self-repair is the ability to mend what has been damaged within you. Yes, finally! Something we can excel at!

Self-repair involves slowing down and taking the time to examine your thoughts and actions. It requires looking at why you say one thing but do another. It's about addressing and challenging these issues so you can develop a plan to work through them. Remember, if we don't identify the issues, we cannot make the necessary changes to resolve them.

Let's start by identifying what you didn't receive from your care-givers. According to child development frameworks, there are eight essential needs that support a child's successful growth into a well-adjusted adult. They are:

- Security & Safety
- Stability
- Affection & Love
- Structure & Consistency
- Emotional Support & Coaching
- Positive Role Models
- Opportunities for Play & Exploration
- Educational Support & Encouragement
- Time & Attention

I've also added a few more to enhance the concept.

1. Security and Safety

Children require a stable environment where their basic needs—such as shelter, food, and protection—are consistently met. This foundational sense of safety enables them to explore and learn without undue fear.

 Children must feel safe and sound, with their basic survival needs met: shelter, food, clothing, medical care, and protection from harm.

— Childrenscolorado.org

2. Affection and Love

Consistent expressions of love and physical affection are vital for emotional development. Such nurturing fosters secure attachments and a healthy self-concept.

 Children who had affectionate mothers were less anxious, emotionally distressed, and less likely to be hostile.

— Awarenessact.com

3. Structure and Consistency

Predictable routines and clear boundaries help children understand expectations, promoting a sense of control and responsibility.

 Children do best when they know what to expect… Structure teaches them time management and sets them up for healthy habits.

— Childrenscolorado.org

4. Emotional Support and Coaching

Guiding children to recognize and manage their emotions equips them with resilience and empathy, essential for interpersonal relationships.

 Kids are not born with the ability to express and manage their emotions. They rely on us to help them do that.

— Awarenessact.com

5. Positive Role Models

Children emulate behaviors observed in adults. Demonstrating empathy, integrity, and perseverance provides a blueprint for their own conduct.

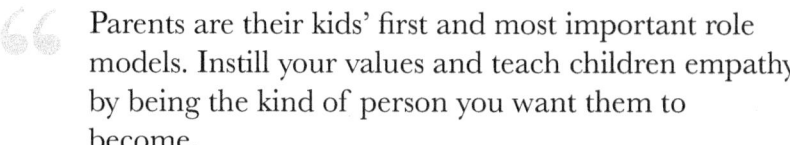

Parents are their kids' first and most important role models. Instill your values and teach children empathy by being the kind of person you want them to become.

— Childrenscolorado.org

6. Opportunities for Play and Exploration

Engaging in play allows children to develop creativity, problem-solving skills, and social understanding.

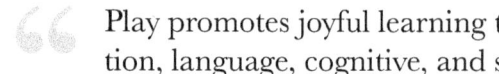

Play promotes joyful learning that fosters self-regulation, language, cognitive, and social competencies.

— Naeyc.org

7. Educational Support and Encouragement

Access to learning resources and encouragement in educational pursuits lays the groundwork for academic success and lifelong learning.

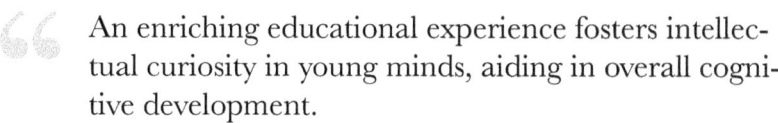

An enriching educational experience fosters intellectual curiosity in young minds, aiding in overall cognitive development.

— Thebeehiveconnection.com

8. Time and Attention

Quality time spent with children reinforces their sense of worth and strengthens the parent-child bond.

 The time you spend with your kids gives you the opportunity to provide your kids all their essential needs — and much more.

— Childrenscolorado.org

Remember, as discussed in previous chapters, how a person's upbringing influences their attachment style. One of the first steps in self-repair is to address your needs. However, to do this, you must first understand what those needs are.

Take a look at the list above and identify three needs that you didn't receive from your caretaker during childhood. Write them down in detail to ensure that parts of your inner child are acknowledged and present.

Now, consider this: if you had consistently received all eight essential needs mentioned earlier during your upbringing, how might your life look different today? Reflect on areas such as physical health, relationships, education or career, finances, spirituality, personal growth, self-expression, community involvement, household management, parenting, and self-care. Would you still be the same version of yourself? Why or why not?

Let's explore how to provide those needs for yourself now—and what that looks like in practice.

Before we dive in, let's discuss reparenting and inner child healing.

Inner child healing and reparenting are techniques designed to heal childhood wounds. These wounds can be emotional or mental and often involve recognizing and understanding the unmet needs from early life. This process includes finding ways to fulfill those needs now, utilizing skills and tools like reparenting.

Reparenting is the process of identifying what you didn't receive as a child and consciously nurturing and validating your own experiences and emotions. You become the caregiver to your younger self.

Have you seen the movie *Little* with Marsai Martin and Taraji P. Henson, where Taraji magically transforms back into her 13-year-old self, played by Marsai? That's you. The idea is that you are now reparenting the 13-year-old version of yourself, which can sometimes be quite challenging.

Do you remember how you were as a child? Now, imagine being in that space again—but without the adult reasoning skills and emotional tools you possess now. That's the visual.

Reparenting involves seeing yourself as that little kid, doing the work to identify what she missed and taking responsibility for providing her with those things now.

And no—I'm not referring to how you weren't allowed to eat Oreos, leading you to overindulge now, thinking that's healing. No, that's not what we're aiming for.

I'm talking about the eight essential needs you've already identified through hard work. You've asked yourself the questions; now it's time to show up and give yourself those things.

Let's go!

What does it look like in practice to provide yourself with the unmet needs from childhood?

I'm glad you asked—let's take a look. You have your list, right?

Let's start with the first one: security and safety. In practice, this means learning to listen to your body. As a woman, if you find yourself in a situation where you feel unsafe—physically or mentally—then you probably shouldn't be there. Trust your intuition.

For example, getting gas at night? That's a no-go for me. However, I do make exceptions—such as at places I've visited multiple times, well-lit areas, or if I'm with someone I trust, someone who has my back. Going to the ATM at night? Another no-go. There might be exceptions, but the goal is to recognize your own limits and boundaries.

It's now your responsibility to consider potential dangers. I'm not saying to live in fear, but I am saying no prince charming is coming to save you. You must learn to save yourself.

Let's also discuss another aspect of safety—being your own source of safety and security. This requires a shift in mindset. It starts with stopping the search for external validation and instead creating that safety for yourself.

This looks like establishing daily routines, moving your body, consistently meeting your own needs, and cultivating inner stability. It's about being so content and whole internally that if someone leaves, you're still home—because you've built a home within yourself. You're no longer abandoning yourself.

Now let's talk about love and affection. (And yes, I know you want to sing the song—"I need love and affection… love, ugh-ugh-ugh… love, ugh-ugh-ugh…" —Rihanna featuring Future).

In this category, giving yourself love and affection in real time could involve understanding the type of love and affection you need. Do you require physical touch? Words of affirmation? Quality time? Receiving gifts? Acts of service?

If you're not familiar with the five love languages, please look them up or read *The 5 Love Languages* by Gary Chapman. This is crucial because you can't change or meet a need if you don't have a name for it.

This may explain why you find yourself in bed with someone, thinking love equals sex, not realizing you just wanted to be touched.

So, let's break down what it actually looks like when you give these things to yourself.

Physical Touch:

Some ways to provide physical touch for yourself include getting a massage or taking a warm oat milk flower bath—yes, make it aesthetically pleasing. Embrace your softer side and give yourself things you once deemed "too girly" or "for other girls." Ask a family member for a hug without saying anything. Hug yourself.

Side note: there was a time I hated my belly. Now, I don't hate it… I'm still working on it to align with my vision, but I started making jokes about myself, like calling myself a "busted can of biscuits" or referencing "talking Betty!" from the movie *White Chicks* with the Wayans. Unbeknownst to me, the little girl in me was listening and filing this away under low self-esteem.

So, I initiated a practice where I hugged my stomach and spoke to it. I told my stomach, "You are one of the best parts of me, and I'm grateful for you." Because whether we admit it or not, our bodies have endured a lot, and we haven't always been kind to them —eating whatever, not getting enough rest, bumping into furniture, stubbing toes, and brushing it off as if it didn't matter—only to wonder where those mystery bruises came from.

I created time and space to express my love for my body. I began a ritual of thanking it for carrying me this far and affirming that I was proud of it for making it through, vowing never to abandon it again.

I established routines—skincare, better hygiene. I started purchasing expensive perfumes, lotions, body scrubs, and creams to care for myself. I didn't just say I loved myself—I showed it. I demonstrated to my body, my younger self, and my future self that I was present and ready to do the work.

Structure and Consistency:

This is where you set a goal and commit to it. Write down five reasons why you deserve your goal, and then jot down five motivations behind those reasons. It's not a matter of if, but when. When hard times arise (and they will), this list will remind you why you started and help you stay on track.

The more structured and consistent you are, the more you will trust and depend on yourself. This helps close the internal split we discussed earlier and reduces self-sacrifice and self-abandonment.

You create routines, write to-do lists, meal prep, and keep your promises to yourself. You become committed to your growth, no matter what. The more consistent you are, the more confidence you gain in taking up space without begging for what you already carry within. WOO HOO—let's go!

Emotional Support and Coaching:

This is important.

As Black people, we often don't engage with emotional support systems. Consequently, many of us have damaged relationships—or none at all. That means you're going to have to be your own emotional support and coach.

This involves giving your feelings a voice. Sit down and identify your mood and emotions. Write them down. Say them out loud so your body, mind, and soul can get used to your voice—and you advocating for yourself.

Ask yourself: What do I need in this moment? Then learn how to provide that need for yourself instead of seeking outside sources to fulfill it.

This is emotional intelligence. You're becoming aware of your feelings, emotions, and moods. Once you identify them, you can communicate and express them healthily.

There will be times you need encouragement and coaching. Talk to yourself like a supportive parent would. I remember once telling myself, It's okay to cry—but cry while walking out that door, because this isn't it!

There was a time I had to coach myself—saying things like, You got this. Keep going. Then I found a song by Deraj Global called "You Got This," which expressed everything I needed to hear. It helped me keep pushing and became an anthem for my self-development and healing. That song—and others like it—became my playlist for rising.

It's funny how we can go so hard for everyone else except ourselves, isn't it?

Okay sis, let's take a breather. Let's check in.

How are you feeling?

Do you notice any physical symptoms? Are there emotions manifesting in your body?

Do you suddenly feel tired, drained, or heavy for no reason?

Yeah… it's working. It's hitting. That's stage one.

If you're not feeling it yet, that's okay too. These feelings can manifest in different ways. Now it's up to you, Ms. Parent, to notice the signs and provide the necessary care.

Let's keep going.

Positive Role Modeling:

This involves doing things today that your future self will be proud of. It means investing in your well-being—putting in time, money, and energy now to reap the benefits later.

It means setting boundaries to build self-respect. For example: We don't fall in love quickly; we fall in love safely. That sets the standard. So when someone comes along who challenges that, you can say: Nope. That's not for me. This is the standard.

Yassss.

It looks like speaking kindly to yourself and checking the inner critic. Model grace, compassion, and love—not punishment, fear, or pain.

It's showing your younger self—who couldn't do anything back then—how to choose herself because you do it now. Because you model it.

It's walking away from people who don't value you—and being okay with that decision. You're now in charge of your emotional, mental, physical, spiritual, and financial care.

Play and Exploration:

This involves being present and enjoying the moment. It's not being ruled by strict black-and-white routines. It's hearing your favorite song and dancing. It's trying something new—like taking that pottery class you've been considering since watching *Ghost*.

Ask yourself: What did I love doing as a kid that I stopped?

It's choosing not to care what others think. It's creating joy on your own terms.

Educational Support and Encouragement:

This looks like asking yourself real questions about your future. Are you satisfied with your career? Do you have unspoken dreams about going back to school or learning something new—but you've been putting it off because it might inconvenience others?

I'm not talking about neglecting responsibilities as a parent, caretaker, or employee.

I'm talking about honoring the whispers of unfulfilled dreams and desires.

This means taking courses or certifications to advance in your career. It means reading and researching topics like abandonment wounds, attachment styles, or borderline personality disorder. Remember—it's LAYERS, and this could be Layer 1 or Layer 35.

It's growing in self-development and doing the things that build your self-esteem and remind you of your worth.

Time and Attention:

This is about prioritizing yourself and your care.

In real time, that looks like saying no to anything that drains you. No more self-sacrificing. No more self-abandoning. It's having a routine—and sticking to it. Not dropping it every time someone calls and asks for a favor.

Sure, helping isn't bad. There's no issue with being there for someone. The issue arises when helping others comes at the cost of abandoning yourself. Eventually, a warning light comes on. A symptom. A flare-up. And that light is saying: Hey sis, you didn't take care of yourself.

So now it's about turning off distractions. Sitting with yourself.

Sitting with your thoughts—not trying to fix them, not running from them—just being okay with being you.

Ask yourself: What do I want to do today?

Then go with your own flow. Take up space in your life—without judgment, guilt, or fear of consequences.

Let this sink in: Healing isn't a finish line. It's a new lifestyle.

Everything you've done so far? It now becomes your new daily rhythm. Your new foundation. Your new normal.

Healing is a daily choice—a choice to choose you.

You're now the one in charge.

Welcome to Reparenting 101:

Let's take a moment to explore healthy attachment styles—how to build secure attachment and what that looks like, especially when you're starting from a place of abandonment.

We've spent most of this journey unpacking what's not healthy: abandonment wounds, trauma, and toxic relationships. Now it's time to shift into what's possible. What does it actually mean to have a healthy attachment? What does it look like in real time?

Secure attachment is rooted in trust, safety, and emotional security. It feels safe to express yourself. There's open communication. The relationship honors and promotes both connection and independence. There's reliability, consistency, and mutual respect.

It's the ability to trust others while maintaining your own identity. It involves setting boundaries and respecting them. It's about forming deep connections and receiving love without guilt, fear, or anxiety.

Once we understand what secure attachment is, we must examine what makes it difficult to achieve—especially after experiencing trauma or abandonment. Let's bring the nervous system into the conversation.

Remember the trauma responses we discussed earlier? Fight, flight, freeze, and fawn—these responses don't just disappear. Even when you want to form secure attachments, your body may still react as if it's under threat. That's why emotional regulation is so critical.

Healing and building secure attachment begins with regulating your emotions in real time. This means validating what you feel, allowing yourself to sit with the discomfort, and working through it —before jumping into reaction-mode behavior.

This process involves slowing down to ask yourself:

- What am I feeling right now?
- What triggered this feeling?
- What do I feel like doing in response?
- What do I actually need in this moment?

Many of those answers might sound like:

- "I need to…"
- "I have to…"
- "I'm afraid that if I don't…"

And that's okay. That's honesty. Learning how you navigate emotions provides insight into your rhythm and flow, helping you become less reactive and more responsive.

Being responsive means pausing, reflecting, and choosing intentional actions based on emotional intelligence—not fear.

After you've identified what you're feeling and articulated it, the next step is to tune in to your body. What is your body saying? Is your heart racing? Are your hands sweaty? Do you feel like someone just punched you in the stomach?

Whatever your physical response is, you need to find a custom-made self-soothing technique to meet it.

For instance, if you're having trouble catching your breath, and it's not an emergency or a full-blown panic attack, try deep breathing or counting to ten. If it's a mind-body-soul response, consider listening to a guided meditation to calm all parts. Write down what you're feeling and give it space. It doesn't have to be true, and it doesn't have to be a lie—it's your emotion. Your emotions are real, and it's valid to feel them. However, ask yourself: how much of what I'm feeling is influenced by fear or negative core beliefs?

Learn to sit with it. Remember, you're the parent now, so it's okay to say things like, "It's going to be okay. You're feeling this because of X. Give it some time and let it pass." This helps reduce reactivity. Learning to breathe through it will calm your nervous system. Sometimes, a good nap works wonders—it can feel like a reset, a refresh, a soft restart.

What do you do when you're feeling overwhelmed? Try grounding yourself—tap your foot or finger, do something small to disrupt the pattern, and give your brain a moment to reorient. Explore therapeutic techniques like somatic therapy or DBT (Dialectical Behavior Therapy), which assist with physical repro-gramming.

Understand this: your body needs repetition to believe that safety is real. Taking a calming bath, working out, or going for a walk are all helpful, but the most effective option—because the body keeps score—is yoga. The movement and stretches help release pain from your body and retrain it to respond differently, without defaulting to high alert or fear.

Daily check-ins and routines can help. They create structure and consistency so that when someone tries to cross a boundary, your healed self will automatically speak up. You won't have to think twice—it will come out naturally. And when it does, you might look back and think, "Did I just say that?" Yes, sis. That was you!

Speak to yourself with compassion, not criticism. The inner environment of safety you create will radiate outward. That doesn't mean people won't challenge you—it just means it won't matter. You've become everything you need.

When you stop neglecting and ghosting your own needs, you find peace. You become more grounded, more whole, more fulfilled—because you're filling your own cup. You recognize emotional neglect when it arises, and instead of spiraling, you respond with love. Creating mantras and affirmations helps both the mind and the body. It provides them with direction and clear command.

Now it's time to unlearn the lies of survival attachment.

It's not a matter of if—it's a matter of when. When you're triggered, when the inner child feels anxious or scared, you cannot ignore it. That's self-abandonment. You must give yourself room to feel and be heard.

Create space and ask:

- What happened?
- What's wrong?
- What can I do to soothe this?

Challenge the belief system behind it. You can say:

- "Yes, they left me. Yes, this happened. But this is not my identity."
- "They chose to leave because they wanted to. That doesn't mean I'm not enough."
- "It's not my job to make someone stay. I don't have that kind of power."
- "I don't have to earn love just to keep it. I can express my needs safely because I now meet my own needs.

Tell yourself:

- "I'm going to take care of you. You don't have to worry anymore. If I can do it for others, surely I can do it for myself."
- "I create the world I want to live in, and with that, I get to decide who stays and who goes."
- "I have the power to manage my emotions and my environment."
- "If someone meant to hurt me, I choose to use it as feedback—not as my identity."

You no longer see life through the lens of abandonment, fear, or pain. You see it through love.

Ask yourself:

- What if what they said came from their own pain?
- What if that behavior was their trauma, not mine?

It's not yours to carry. But it is your responsibility to protect your emotional space. It's not your job to decipher someone else's thoughts, feelings, or behavior. Your job is to decipher your own— and to do so with grace. You're still learning. You're human.

These realizations become your boundaries, not your barriers.

They allow you to say what needs to be said without guilt, shame, or shrinking. You'll stand on the truth that what's for you is already yours. You don't have to earn it. You don't have to over-function for it. You don't have to be anyone other than your healed, whole, real self.

Now, I'm not saying you should go through life just waiting for things to drop into your lap, but you are no longer responsible for chasing or fixing. You understand now that the people who are meant for you will have the capacity to hold you, so being misunderstood no longer defines you. Either way, you're not afraid of it anymore. You've learned that, at the end of the day, people will feel, think, and believe what they want about you, and most of the time, there's nothing you can do to change that. Eventually, it will never be enough, and that's only because those people were never for you.

Learning the difference between intimacy and intensity will help you recognize what's safe and allow you to receive it. This will be a challenge, but it's part of the process. Working on understanding safety, security, who to trust, and what to trust makes it hard to receive love when it finally comes. Why? Because deep down, you still believe that you have to go through something for love to be real. But once you let go of that and understand that how and when love comes doesn't matter, you'll be able to enjoy the present moment.

Since you are no longer in charge of fixing, you're not concerned about all the ways things could go wrong. That frees you up to focus on yourself. Managing your thoughts, emotions, and reactions is already enough to handle. Freeing yourself from trying to control every possible outcome will give you the strength to understand that you can only control what you can control—and that is you.

When you feel safe, the situation is safe because you are your safety. You're not handing your heart to someone at a discount. If and when things don't work out, you no longer spiral—you shift. You no longer dwell on the past or try to fix things just to validate your unhealed abandonment wounds.

Remember, you can't control anyone. You can't control the outcome of a situation. And you can't magically make everything work in your favor. It's about detaching from being the only responsible one and stepping into being responsible for your actions alone.

Releasing the addiction to potential is key. You're no longer attracted to potential—you live in the now. The only potential you're invested in is the endless possibilities of your own life. That's what you can control. What you do and how you do it will determine your path.

Know this: secure love will feel kind of boring. You may itch for some form of toxicity or chaos to make love feel like what you once thought it was. But trust—your soul will feel safe. Your inner child will let go. You'll become the safe space you used to look for in others.

Now, let's explore how to rewire how you receive love.

You do know that you have the right to set the tone, the standard, and the pace in your romantic life, right? You do it in every other area—so why not in love? Oh, you didn't know that? Well, I'm here to tell you: you can. And you don't need anyone's permission.

Of course, it's going to be hard to let people love you—because all your life you've had to fight (Color Purple reference, yes!). But now you have to stop fighting yourself in order to receive it.

How do you do that? You let people show you who they are. You let them show up for you. If someone asks, "Are you okay?" "What can I do to support you?" "What are your needs?"—you don't brush it off. You don't prove that you don't need them. You take up space. And you let someone else take up space with you.

Of course, this comes with layers—you've deemed them trust-worthy, reliable, consistent, and willing to do the work. And then? You let them love you. You let that man be a man.

When you're dating and he's going through hard times, and you feel the urge to fix it, overcompensate, or take over—you address that. Tell yourself, "That ain't your man, sis!" Remind yourself of your boundaries: what you will and won't do, what's your responsibility, and what's not.

Practice saying things in the mirror like, "Good morning, beautiful," or "How are you feeling today?" Check in with yourself and your body. That way, when someone else offers compliments or kindness, you won't feel like you have to earn it. You'll already know: you deserve it.

You're supposed to receive good treatment. You're supposed to be cherished and valued. Anything less? Not for you. This isn't an uppity attitude—it's a right attitude.

When you believe you deserve love and care, you expect it. And when you expect it, it doesn't surprise you—you won't feel like you have to work or hustle for it. It becomes the standard.

That changes how you see yourself. It changes how you show up in the world. It changes how you date.

Dating now looks like choosing people who are consistent, responsive, and emotionally available—not just "he's 6ft," "he's kind to his momma," or "he goes to church." It looks like you being calm and attuned to your emotions, no longer confusing chemistry and chaos with connection and intimacy.

You notice you're no longer performing. You know you are enough. And if someone doesn't see your value? You don't panic. You don't hustle harder. You don't beg to stay.

Because you've finally realized—the people who are for you won't need convincing.

Yes, there will be times when things won't go as planned, when you're not someone's type, or when you don't fit their mold. And that's okay. You have preferences too. That's also okay. But your worth? It's not defined by what you do, what you give, or who wants or rejects you.

Your worth is defined by you.

Some *green flags* to start you on your way include:

- They repair after conflict
- They honor your pace
- They celebrate your voice, not just your silence
- They value and support independence

Now, let's talk about actively creating secure attachments in relationships. This can look like choosing partners who can regulate their emotions and have the ability and willingness to co-regulate—meaning they have the emotional maturity to support you in regulating your emotions. It looks like choosing a person who can communicate and express their needs and set clear boundaries. It looks like building together—where one person is not responsible for carrying the entire weight of the relationship. It also means both parties know their worth and are able to leave or walk away from something that is no longer serving them.

A "Safe Love Checklist" (behaviors and traits of a securely attached partner):

- Follows through
- Accepts feedback
- Honors boundaries
- Doesn't punish your vulnerability

Healing from abandonment isn't just about the inner work. It's about unlearning survival tactics that keep you disconnected from secure attachment relationships. Having a community and support system is important. With anything you go through, it's hard to do it alone. But often, people who suffer from abandonment wounds don't have many friends due to a lack of trust and fear of being hurt if they let someone in. Changing this is the beginning of security.

Having people you can be vulnerable with forms the foundation of healing. The idea is to create safety. Again, we do the work by ensuring that the people we give access to are deemed worthy—through time and efforts that prove it. In this process, you will learn safety, trust, and love again.

I truly believe, based on my Christian views and my relationship with God and Jesus, that relationships were created to help us experience life. They foster our growth, provide love and support, and challenge the aspects of our lives that are not right. In fact, if it weren't for that heartbreak, would you have even recognized your abandonment wounds?

Sometimes, relationships act as magnifying glasses—they reveal what has been hidden and what needs to be addressed. Some people may think they are healed when they self-isolate, take time for themselves, and shut off the world, but in reality, they have merely stopped. It's often when they re-enter a relationship that they realize those unresolved issues are still present; now, someone is there to poke at them and bring them to the surface.

It's important to cultivate friendships that honor your journey of becoming. Seek a therapist who provides support and offers truthful feedback without shame. Engaging in self-healing opens the door; however, safe relationships guide you through it.

Let's discuss what a safe community offers—just in case you're thinking, "I'm fine, I don't need anyone." That still sounds a bit like hurt.

A safe community or support system provides:

- Presence
- Understanding/ Empathy
- Consistency
- Accountability

These are the ingredients of safe, secure attachment.

A therapeutic relationship becomes a sacred rehearsal for secure love because, in therapy, you learn to name and process your trauma and abandonment wounds. You learn to sit with your emotions and rewire them—with guided support. You create and practice healthy boundaries and communication in a safe environment. You also learn how to heal your nervous system and co-regulate your emotions in real time.

Some real-time practices for healing within a community include:

- Joining a support group (on Facebook, Instagram, or local meetups)
- Attending therapy regularly
- Making connections with people in your community (such as at your church or gym)
- Saying yes to being seen

This might look like joining a workout boot camp—where instead of shying away and shrinking, you choose to make connections. These are the initial stages of healing in real time. This is what it looks like to build a secure life, one step at a time.

Station 10

The Re-Fluff Table

Welcoming Back the One Who Was Never Meant to Disappear

This station is about restoration. Not of a relationship but of the version of you that got buried beneath survival, performance, and unmet needs. It's time to re-fluff the parts of you that became flat from constantly showing up for others while forgetting yourself.

Real self-love isn't performative it's protective. It's reflected in your rest, your rhythms, your standards, and your silence. This chapter invites you to stop seeking what you already carry within. Because when you truly believe you are worthy, you no longer overextend, explain, or negotiate your value.

Welcome back the version of you who was never broken only buried. She's been waiting for your return.

*   *   *

When I mentioned that rest is a part of recovery and self-care in the previous chapter, I could almost see your eyes widen in disbelief. That should have been a clear indicator of how little you actually care for yourself. If we were to step back and examine your actions —not just what you tell yourself—would you honestly say that you truly love yourself?

If he didn't speak at all, how could you know he loves you? What are some indicators that he cherishes you?

Self-care is more than just getting your nails done, dining out, or taking bubble baths. It encompasses the actions you take to care for yourself. These actions are necessities for you to be the best version of yourself. It means going to bed on time, being mindful of what you eat and how it makes you feel, and being selective about who you allow into your life—and to what extent. These are all signs of self-worth and feeling safe within yourself. It's when you stop asking for what you already possess. It's when you no longer negotiate your worth, especially with those who lack the capacity to understand or love you properly.

What would life look like if you gave yourself just 10% of what you give to that man or family? Who would you become if you supported yourself and acted as your own best friend? We both know you go all out for your loved ones. In fact, when you enter a room, or when others know you're involved in something, they automatically feel reassured because they know you will come through no matter what.

If only you had yourself as a support system. If only you had yourself as a friend! Nothing could stop you from achieving whatever you wanted. It would be game over for everyone else!

You are unstoppable. If only you could direct that energy toward yourself.

The truth is, because you lack self-love, self-worth, and self-care, your wounds remain open. If you gave yourself just a fraction of what you give others, there would be no feelings of abandonment or self-neglect. When you don't love yourself, you pour all that love and energy into others—proving and overcompensating. When that love is rejected, it extinguishes the hope within you. It dries up like a desert, leaving you vulnerable to mirages that arise from delusion and neglect.

This is where the therapeutic action of reparenting comes in. It's about giving yourself what you didn't receive in childhood. You nurture yourself so that you can become a nurturer. When you need rest, you don't beat yourself up for not being Superwoman. You grab your heating pad, soak your feet, and watch *Waiting to Exhale* all by yourself. You validate your pain and give it a voice instead of shutting it down, ignoring it, or pushing past your limits just to avoid being seen as weak or unreliable.

You create safety within your own body by hugging yourself, getting massages, or doing Pilates—instead of seeking a touch that leaves you feeling emptier than before. You speak kindly to yourself. You confront that inner critic by asking why, when, and what now— instead of avoiding it and spiraling later when something doesn't go your way.

When you love yourself, you recognize red flags more quickly and can make informed decisions about how to address them. Not from a place of hurt or fear, but from a position of knowing that you already have everything you need and don't have to chase what's rightfully yours.

Think about it: Do you chase your bills? No, they know exactly where you live, have your name on them, and show up on time every month. Do you chase your house key or the place where you live? No—you simply walk up, unlock the door, and step into your space. This is the same for what belongs to you—it will flow into your life effortlessly.

No more chasing.

No more fixing.

No more proving.

Just safe love.

Embracing your value to rebuild self-esteem and learn to love yourself unconditionally is the most important part. As I've said before—and many times—how you see yourself and how you present yourself in the world determines the life you lead. Your beliefs and perceptions influence your behavior. If you don't value yourself or believe in your worth, it doesn't matter what coping skills you employ, what conversations you have, or what others may say— it will ultimately crumble if you don't see it for yourself.

So, let's rebuild that and break free from this toxic environment. Let's go!

First and foremost—what is self-esteem?

Let's discuss how you perceive yourself. I know we touched on this before, but let's delve deeper. Self-esteem is confidence. Confidence is belief. It's the assurance and trust, mingled with a bit of faith and reliance—either on others or on yourself.

Having self-esteem means having assurance, hope, belief, and faith in yourself. It's not just about what you can do; it's more about who you are and being proud of that.

To cultivate self-esteem, you need confidence. That means believing in yourself—believing that you are worthy and capable.

If you need proof, consider this: What are three things you've overcome in the last 60 days?

Exactly. You're amazing.

Often, because we are so close to our situations, we only see the cracks and don't step back to see the bigger picture. Right now, you are in Chapter 10 of this book. Do you realize how dedicated and committed to yourself you must be to have made it this far?

That is proof that you want the best for yourself and that you believe. So why not believe in you?

And if you need a reminder, here it is:

You made it. Yes, you!

You made it through the hurt, the abandonment, the rejection— and you're still here.

You may not be completely put together, but you are here—and with my book! That's significant.

And I see you, sis—because I am you.

Loving yourself is more than just words or getting your hair done. It's reflected in how you allow people to treat you, how you permit them to talk to you, what you prioritize, and the actions you take to care for your body, mind, soul, emotions, and finances.

That is love. That is action. When you do that, you learn to love yourself through the mistakes, the growth, the hardships—and all the in-between—without conditions and without needing to prove your worth.

You learn to nurture, show up, protect, and appreciate yourself. This builds your self-perception, which boosts your confidence—and that confidence enhances your self-esteem.

It helps you manage well and understand your weaknesses without fearing them. You can slow down and ask yourself questions like:

What happened here?

How did this affect me?

You'll be able to identify triggers that impact your self-esteem and adjust—not tear yourself down. Because we already know: you can't heal what you're afraid to name or identify.

Here are some practical steps you can take in real-time to rebuild your self-esteem:

1. Celebrate yourself and your efforts.

As I mentioned earlier, you've overcome challenges that you may perceive as small or insignificant. That's often because you were only praised when something worked out or yielded results that benefited others. We're no longer doing that.

2. Practice building evidence.

Start journaling. Keep a record. Take pictures. Write things down.

Let me tell you something: if there's one thing the mind will do—it's lie. Your brain might say: "You aren't really doing anything. You might as well stay in bed." "You're still not healed. Just stop—this isn't working." But then you stop. You sit there and look back…

Then, you review those pictures and journals and realize—
Who lied to me?! Yeah… you did. Well, your brain did.
Because it was trying to stay comfortable. It didn't want to
change. It didn't believe in your potential.

3. Replace criticism with curiosity.

This creates space for you to learn. This is the first time
you're really applying pressure to yourself—so choose
progress over perfection. No more viewing mistakes as
personal failures. Process them in a safe space. Ask questions.
No more linking your mistakes to your identity. That's not
who you are. You're learning. You're growing.

One reason this can be challenging is that you're older now.
Often, that means being stubborn and set in your ways. But that was
the old you. We're progressing toward the healed version of yourself
every day.

Remember: when you are present with yourself, you can identify
and express your emotions in real-time. You can validate your feelings without needing someone else to do it for you.

Understand this: Self-love isn't a feeling—it's a daily practice.
Healing isn't linear—it's layered. So, don't let setbacks derail your
momentum.

From one of my favorite coaches who helped me through difficult times and became my audible Bible for a season—Les Brown:
"You don't have to be **GREAT** to get started, but you have to get
started to be **GREAT!**"

What does living this out in real-time look like?

- Not fearing healthy people—but boldly positioning
  yourself to attract them.
- Advocating for yourself—even when your voice shakes.
- Wearing clothes that make you feel your best—because
  you are worth it.

- Surrounding yourself with people who reflect your value back to you.

Let me be clear: loving yourself doesn't mean life won't be hard. It doesn't mean people won't disappoint you. And it doesn't mean you'll never hurt again.

It means that in this chapter of your life, you are being intentional about you. It is your responsibility to protect, provide for, and care for yourself. You are not a project to be fixed. Not every day has to be about self-improvement. Sometimes, it's simply a day to enjoy the journey.

Enjoy the fresh batch of roses on your dining room table—the ones you bought for yourself because you discovered that you truly love flowers. The world may not have taught you how to value yourself, but now, you have the opportunity to become the woman who will.

Station 11

The Final Stitch

No Is the Needle, Peace Is the Pattern —
Sealing What's Sacred

In this final station, we seal the sacred work. The stitches of your healing journey are held together by one essential thread: boundaries. Saying no is not rejection it's restoration. It is the needle that repairs the unraveling, and peace is the pattern that emerges when you stop bending for what doesn't serve you.

This chapter offers practical tools to create emotional safety first within yourself, then in your relationships. Boundaries are not walls; they are sacred instructions for how others are allowed to engage with the masterpiece you're becoming. Like maintaining a well-loved car, this is the work that keeps your soul running smoothly and your spirit protected.

You are no longer waiting to be rescued. You are responsible for your care, your energy, and your peace. And beloved, that kind of love the kind you give yourself is the most sacred stitch of all.

* * *

There are several categories of boundaries to consider, but we will focus on four. The first is *emotional boundaries*, which protect your feelings. If someone is gaslighting you or making you feel invalidated, this is a violation of that boundary. This is often one of the first signs of manipulation. If they can silence your voice through gaslighting, the rest becomes easier for them.

The next category is *mental boundaries*, which involve guarding your thoughts, beliefs, and time for reflection. This means standing up for your thoughts without arguing over them—being firm and not allowing yourself to be manipulated. Once someone makes you feel like your thoughts are merely emotional or untrue, they will have you questioning every idea, undermining your confidence and self-esteem. This dynamic leads to power, control, and manipulation, ultimately resulting in abuse.

Next, we have *physical boundaries*, which honor your body and personal space. For example, if you don't feel like being touched at the moment, you have the right to express that and change the situation. You do not have to continue something just because it has already begun; if you feel uncomfortable, you can walk away from any space that doesn't feel right for you. Recall the previous chapter, where we discussed the importance of feeling safe and listening to your gut and intuition—that was part of establishing physical boundaries.

Finally, *spiritual boundaries* involve respecting your faith, values, and sacred time. This means standing up for what you believe in, prioritizing what is important to you, and being committed to the time you designate for your spiritual connection.

Let's address what boundary violations look like. It can manifest as someone making you feel guilty for choosing to go to church instead of a birthday party you were invited to. It's when you tell someone to stop squeezing your leg because it's uncomfortable, and they forget and do it again and again. It's being consistently ignored or dismissed. It's having your emotions invalidated, being told you're too sensitive, too extra, called a "drama queen," or being labeled as "just so emotional." It's when you neglect your own time to overextend yourself in order to avoid conflict or rejection.

So why does this feel like it's going to be hard to change? Well, it is! There will be some angry people around when you start to love yourself, sister. They will not like that you care about yourself because it takes attention away from them. They have no problem with you being unhealed because your people-pleasing benefited them. Often, they don't even realize they are behaving this way. They may say things like, "I guess you're brand new, huh?" or "Oh, you think you're all that, huh? Well, excuse me, Ms. 'I love myself'!" These are all tests and triggers designed to make you back down and revert to people-pleasing, making you feel like the relationship is threatened. In reality, it is threatened because you are not the same anymore. The old you has left the building, and the new you is not having it. They may struggle to accept the new you, but remember what we discussed earlier: the people who are meant for you will support your evolution.

You don't have to prove to them that you are the same, that you have their back, or that you won't leave them. In fact, they will love your growth and support it! Let those who remain attached to the old version of you stay where they are, at a level they can handle, because the new you requires more, and they may not have what it takes to maintain a relationship. Even if they do catch up, by the time they get there, you will have healed another part of yourself and will have moved on.

Some other common struggles you may encounter include feeling selfish or mean for saying no. Let me share something I learned long ago: for every time you tell someone no, you are telling yourself yes. This means that when you say no, you are protecting your peace, time, and energy. Everything should come from a place of overflow and abundance. If you give up your time and energy, you will soon find that you have nothing left. This can spiral out of control quickly; you may notice yourself declining, with moods shifting, becoming easily frustrated, emotionally drained, and less motivated.

Have you ever seen someone give from a place of abundance? It's different, isn't it? It feels more peaceful, free, and supportive. Now, consider someone who gives from their last resources. They may seem a little dry and become resentful. They might not want to give, but they do it anyway for various reasons. This can make you feel like you owe them something, creating a cycle of undying loyalty and people-pleasing until the debt has been paid.

Remember, the people meant for you will honor your limits. So what are some steps to create boundaries for emotional safety? First, you must do the work. Sit down and figure out your needs. What do you need to feel safe? What does safety look and feel like to you? Can you describe it physically, emotionally, mentally, and spiritually? For example, where do you feel the safest, and why? What does this place provide in terms of physical, emotional, mental, or spiritual safety? These aspects need to be protected because they are essential to your everyday life. Protecting them is crucial for becoming the best version of yourself and creating secure attachments with yourself. This must be guarded with all your strength.

For instance, if one thing that makes you feel safe, seen, and understood is waking up every morning and taking care of your emotional needs—writing down how you feel, sitting with those feelings, validating them, and regulating your emotions—then you need to prioritize that. If you stay out all night partying, it will be hard to wake up early and have enough time for self-care. You might find yourself getting up just 20 minutes before you need to leave, rushing out the door. If this pattern continues, you may stop taking care of yourself altogether or do just enough to get by, which is survival mode.

You might feel pressured to stay late at work, and friends may constantly ask you to go out because they think you've been acting differently. You may start to feel guilty about it. So now it's time to recalibrate and focus on recovery care. Recovery care includes activities you enjoy and that provide you with rest—such as long walks in the park, where you feel connected to nature; self-care routines; taking longer baths; or doing an "everything shower" (where you wash your hair, shower, shave, and maintain your beauty). This also means communicating with your family, friends, or job that you won't be going out tonight or staying late. You don't have to provide detailed reasons, but for those with a closer connection to you, it's good to let them know that you need this time to recharge and care for yourself, so you won't be engaging in extracurricular activities outside of your existing commitments.

Acknowledge your limitations and capacity by being honest with yourself and paying attention to your body. Understand this: you are not responsible for managing someone else's emotions or feelings, but you are responsible for managing your own emotions, feelings, and behaviors. The next step is deciding on consequences if necessary. Some people don't learn unless they face consequences. That is their responsibility, not yours, because you set a boundary, and they feel they don't have to abide by it. You get to decide the consequences; it doesn't always mean cutting people off.

I'll tell you, some people love to get rid of others, saying things like "I'm protecting my peace," but without making any changes or taking accountability. A consequence can simply be removing yourself from a situation or having a firm conversation about it. There are many options; it's up to you, Boss Lady. It's best to practice setting boundaries with yourself first before holding others accountable for the boundaries you establish. Trust me, a manipulator can spot a newcomer easily. They will call you out and make you feel like you're not following your own rules while expecting them to follow yours.

So, you want to keep your word, just as you did when you were trying to save that relationship. No shade, but a little truth there. Create self-check-ins to prevent burnout or guilt while maintaining your boundaries, so you won't be manipulated or gaslighted. This will also help you keep your emotions in check, allowing you to understand your reasons and not crumble under pressure. Remember, setting boundaries is not about keeping people away; it's about taking care of you. When you honor your boundaries, you are telling yourself that you are important, smart, and kind. You are affirming to yourself and the world that you matter and will not be disrespected.

In this next section, I want to discuss shifting your narrative— changing the story you tell yourself about yourself, love, and relationships. The goal is to recognize your stories so that you can rewrite them. This is important because, as we discussed in previous chapters, your inner story or narrative shapes your identity, self-worth, and, for the purpose of this book, your relationships.

What does shifting the narrative look like? Before the shift, you might have dated and chosen people based on trauma and feelings of abandonment. You used to respond reactively rather than reflectively. Shame, self-sabotage, and perfectionism kept you stuck in cycles. You didn't believe love was for you, and you settled for what was easy and available.

So, what does life look like after the shift? Imagine a place where you speak from a position of abundance and wholeness, rather than from your wounds. You can respond with intention and grace, fully aware of your presence, voice, and needs.

How do we shift the narrative in real time? There are some steps we can follow, so let's go through them.

Step one: know the story. Often, we react without understanding the triggers behind our actions. It's crucial to slow down and comprehend the "why" behind your feelings and beliefs. Once you identify your narrative, you can catch those thoughts in real time, potentially stopping yourself from saying or doing something impulsive. For instance, if you walk into a room and feel everyone looking at you, you might think, "Here we go, it's always someone out here…" Before you say anything else, pause and push that thought aside; now is not the time or place. Later, when you're in the car, reflect on it and ask yourself, "Whose voice was that—mine, my family's, my past, or his?" If you can recognize this in real time, that's even better.

Ask yourself the same questions: "Whose voice is this?" Take five slow breaths to help calm your emotions and regulate your nervous system, creating space to process instead of react. After identifying the source of that voice and calming yourself, replace the old narrative with a more healing and empowered one. You might say, "I looked really good that night; of course, I drew attention. I am that girl." In real time, affirm, "Of course they are looking at me right now; why not? I am that girl, and I have always been that girl." This helps build your confidence and, in turn, your self-esteem.

Now it's time to embody this new narrative. What does that look like? It means standing tall when you walk in—heel, toe, heel, toe—and smiling. You're not asking for permission to be there; you already belong. Combine that confidence with self-assurance, and you become unstoppable. You must believe in yourself, and once you do, you will respond in alignment with your new narrative.

Let's go over what you will need for this to be effective. First and foremost, you need awareness. You can't address something if you're unaware of its existence or the damage it's causing. Awareness is crucial for recognizing the old narrative and understanding when it awakens or lingers. You will need self-compassion, as this journey can be challenging and slippery. Sometimes it's easier to stick with your familiar patterns, but in the long run, you must consider the cost to your mental and emotional well-being.

You will need to learn how to speak to yourself with kindness and compassion. Create affirmations, practice reframing quickly, and develop counter-narratives for when the old story tries to resurface. Surround yourself with reliable people who can help keep you accountable. They will also serve as mirrors, reflecting back the truth when things get tough and you feel like giving up.

In this process of growth, maintain an open mind and a receptive heart. The goal is to avoid letting your past experiences and abandonment issues keep you stuck in a loop. Remember, you are living, which means you are actively making decisions and experiencing life. Your narrative is a living entity; it is not a final draft. Stay open to healing and willing to edit your story repeatedly as you evolve. The goal is not to arrive at a destination but to continue evolving.

When challenges arise, view them as opportunities for growth. If a situation doesn't go as planned, see it as a chance to stretch and learn. If you meet someone and the relationship starts well but doesn't end the way you hoped, that's okay. At this stage, you should be able to end things peacefully, without acting out, blaming yourself, or spiraling. You can leave a situation with grace, taking with you what you learned, and not waiting for the other shoe to drop out of fear.

When you do leave, you're not trying to reclaim what you invested or retaliate. You leave knowing you are enough, and if it didn't work out, that person simply wasn't meant for you. Both of you can part amicably, recognizing that what was shared came from a place of abundance, not lack.

Fearing change means you are afraid of growth and being stretched, but it also prevents you from experiencing the next version of yourself—the one filled with more truth, life, and love. The next step in this new narrative work is protecting it—setting boundaries. If you don't protect your growth, you risk losing it.

You wouldn't let an eight-year-old drive a car, right? Similarly, you must safeguard what you've worked hard to achieve. This can involve daily grounding practices, such as journaling your thoughts and emotions. Keeping a log is essential, as our minds can trick us into believing we aren't making progress and that it's easier to give up.

The tricky part is that the mind may tell you things like, "You're not going to achieve that," or "You might as well indulge." Then, when you do indulge, it might say, "See, now you're stuck in the same place; you'll be here forever." At this point, it's about choosing your hard. It's hard when you don't take action, which leads to mental and emotional pain, and it's hard when you do take action, which can create stress or physical discomfort.

Understanding that it's going to be hard either way empowers you to choose your hard. You must begin to ask yourself why you seek a relationship. Is it for love, for companionship, or just to help with bills? Often, we pursue things we don't truly desire. What you really seek is safe presence, emotional support, and someone to say, "I've got you," without needing to prove your worth.

When you understand your "why," you can maintain and protect your new narrative. You are the author of your story, and this may be your first chapter, grounded in awareness. It's about taking a stand and no longer letting abandonment define you or scare you into making choices you don't truly want. This marks the beginning of your becoming, and that is the beauty of this journey!

To let go of old beliefs, particularly core beliefs, involves a similar process. First, identify the old belief and ask yourself questions like: Who told me this? Why? When did it start? Next, confront the belief by creating a safe space to explore it. Ask yourself, is this really true, or could there be other factors at play that I'm unaware of? After this reflection, you may need to grieve it. For example, some beliefs may be tied to a loved one, a specific experience, a place, or a particular time in your life. You might also need to grieve the person you were and the future you thought you would have. This can be difficult and may take time. Remember, it's a layered process! Grief is about honoring past events, recognizing what could have been, and accepting what is now. It's about allowing those feelings to take up space and laying them to rest, so they don't resurface years later unexpectedly. You will learn to release the beliefs and the factors that reinforced them. Healing is not possible if you are continuously triggered by what harmed you. You must take action to let go of toxic environments and relationships that keep you tied to your old stories. This can involve setting clear boundaries and breaking patterns that perpetuate the old you, such as over-functioning, over-explaining, or self-sacrificing. A boundary might involve having a conversation with someone to explain that in your current life, you are no longer shrinking yourself to gain acceptance. You can express, "I love you and want to keep you in my life, but I can't afford to dim my light to make you comfortable anymore."

Cognitive reframing can also be beneficial; this involves finding new perspectives and asking yourself what else could be true about the situation. Create scripts or mantras to counteract negative or outdated beliefs. Use emotional awareness by naming the feelings associated with the old belief. Practice replacement, where you substitute the emotions you used to feel with new ones. For instance, if you used to be afraid to express your needs, focus on feeling confident in them and expressing them freely. Another strategy is to move your body in ways that embody your new beliefs, such as practicing walking in heels, dressing for the life you want, and holding your head high as you enter spaces. Act as if you belong because you do!

To maintain and protect this new identity, read books that align with your new beliefs, such as *"The Gifts of Imperfection" by Brené Brown,* which I read annually. Watch TED Talks on vulnerability, identity, or trauma recovery, featuring speakers like Brené Brown, Nadine Burke Harris, and Resmaa Menakem. Consider working with a counselor or coach who can help reframe trauma-based thinking into love-based living.

This process goes beyond merely shutting people out or creating positive affirmations. It involves the art of rewriting your internal core beliefs, narratives, and even the agreements you never realized you made. It's about cultivating environments that support your truth and gently exposing yourself to new possibilities until they feel safe, familiar, and fully embodied. This requires intentionality, motivation, and a willingness to do the work.

Now, let's discuss unseen agreements or unspoken contracts. We touched on this before, but let's delve deeper. To form new beliefs, we must uproot the old ones, but what about the unspoken ones? These are the unconscious agreements made during childhood, trauma, or even everyday experiences. They might manifest as undying loyalty to someone you just met because they brought you flowers when no one else had. They can look like keeping parts of yourself hidden, sharing only what feels safe and withholding other aspects. These contracts were meant for protection but result in limiting beliefs, keeping you in a self-imposed prison while you strive for freedom. This reflects the saying, "Say one thing and do another." It's a subconscious promise to survive, yet it ultimately holds you back.

So, what does creating internal safety look like, and how can you use this new safety to embrace new truths? It involves believing that it's safe to welcome good things, visualizing yourself healed, and embracing the new truth. Seeing someone else receive what you desire can help open you up to the possibility for yourself. However, if you remain surrounded by minimal experiences, it will be challenging to see and accept this for yourself. This requires expanding your perspective and looking outside your comfort zone. You must identify and actively search for the new truth.

When I began this work, I was in the early stages of healing, and now I'm living the life I envisioned 3-5 years ago. I'm actively going through my clothes and shoes, cultivating the life I want to lead. It's hard because I'm still attached to old lifestyles and the lies that suggest I must fit into something that no longer serves me. Let it go; that moment has passed, and this new body deserves clothing that reflects its freedom, evolution, and confidence. You'll need to change your environments, both physical and digital, including social media platforms like Facebook and Instagram. You may need to delete certain connections, old photos, and unfollow accounts to alter the algorithm affecting your mindset.

What does a boundary look like in this context? It means telling yourself you will no longer engage in spaces that expect you to perform, shrink, or prove your worth. Maintenance for this process might involve recording your journey. You can journal your experiences or, if you find writing painful, use your phone for notes or record videos capturing moments when your new beliefs prove true. To protect your mind from spiraling, use boundary affirmations to remind yourself of the cost of old beliefs and the benefits of your new beliefs. Say things like, "I will not allow my mind to trick me into revisiting a mindset I had to heal, only to return to the same pain." Remember that the pain you felt was real, and the lies telling you it wasn't that bad or that it's better to revert to old patterns are just that—lies.

This journey will be challenging, but on the other side of this difficulty lies a beautiful relationship with yourself and the world, and a new way of showing up in life. You'll need to develop a habit of speaking back to your fears and challenging them. Don't let fear run wild; revisit your "why." If you don't have it at the forefront of your mind, it can give pain and confusion the opportunity to mislead you. So, it's crucial to engage in the work previously mentioned. Journal, journal, journal—this is your new baby. Whether through writing or recording, the goal is to track your progress and evidence of change.

Understand that adopting new beliefs takes time. You must believe in yourself and recognize that you deserve this transformation. Be patient as you nurture this journey, and you will notice your nervous system calming, your confidence building, your self-esteem rising, and your life shifting. Remember, building and releasing a belief isn't about forgetting who you are or who you were; it's about reconnecting with who you've always been beneath the abandonment wound.

In previous chapters, I asked you to consider what your life would look like without this wound. How would you live? How would you love? Would you be the same person today? Letting go is an act of trust. You are allowed to outgrow people, places, patterns, and pain. Welcome to your BECOMING!

Station 12

The Return Policy

Custom-Built: No Exchanges, No Refunds, No Re-Entries: What's Healed Can't Be Returned

B y the time you arrive here, something within you has shifted. This isn't just the end of a book it's a reflection point. A moment to honor the journey you've taken back to yourself. You didn't skim through healing you leaned into it. And that matters.

This final station isn't about tying things up in a neat bow. It's about recognizing that once you've reclaimed your worth, there's no negotiating it again. You're not the same woman who began this journey. You no longer have to run, hustle for love, or prove your value through performance or perfection. You've peeled back the layers, faced your fears, and given yourself permission to stop surviving and start living.

What you've built within yourself can't be undone. Not by a past version of you, not by him, not by anyone. You are the return policy firm, whole, and non-refundable.

* * *

If you've made it to this chapter, sis, you didn't just read—you showed up for yourself! I am proud of you. I know that this book has been triggering for you. You know why? Because it has triggered me too. However, through writing this book, I have been able to see my growth in real time, remember my worth, and make it tangible.

You see, when you're working on yourself, it often leads to a mindset of "What's next? Okay, I've got that—so what's next?" Because of this, I haven't allowed anything to sit and manifest. I was still in survival mode, trying to fix things and hustling—constantly moving on to the next task.

Writing this book helped me realize that I no longer have to run. I may not have "made it," but I like to say I've made it out of that mindset. If I hadn't escaped survival mode and recognized that something was wrong, I would still be reacting out of hurt. It took my daughter getting older for me to see that I was hiding behind her. I focused all my attention on raising her and neglected myself. I was convinced that if I gave her enough love—or more than I had —I could fix myself through her success. But I was wrong. At the time, I had no clue. But now, saying it out loud—I see.

Self-awareness is powerful and essential for change. Choosing from a place of love and self-worth transforms everything. You are no longer the woman with the hurt little girl inside. You are not the same. By this chapter, you've grown in your mindset; you are no longer the woman who first picked up this book.

Let me reintroduce myself for those who didn't know:

My name is Monique R. Darnell, and I am a woman of faith who believes that love is the answer. I walk with empathy and under-standing, alongside clear self-worth and self-esteem. I no longer suffer from abandonment wounds, and they no longer dictate my choice of partners. I have arrived at a place where I know who I am.

Your turn—let me hear it. *Yes— that's it!*

No more confusion, ambiguity, survival mode, or performing worthiness. It's about bravery, courage, confidence, and curiosity! You have gone through an intense healing process, and you are still standing. You've awakened the nurturing side of you to be intentional about your self-care. You've become aware of the cycles you were stuck in—such as inherited patterns, church hurt, toxic love, and abuse.

The moment you called out that wound or connected with some of the examples in this book, you broke something. You are no longer who you were when the pain first hit. You're no longer trying to survive and avoid that hurt—coping with pain by trying out various scenarios until you find one with the least discomfort.

You are now BECOMING.

No more fear of what happened to you that kept you in shame, causing you to settle and compromise—or, in this case, build-a-bae-r to fill your emptiness. Now, you're choosing from a healed self!

There is strength in knowing yourself deeply and compassionately. It's empowering! All the self-care you've invested has brought you to a place of self-confidence. You now know the truth and can move accordingly. Knowing yourself isn't wrong—it's strength. Because now, you can't lie to yourself. It's liberation. You can put measures in place to prevent yourself from falling for things that don't serve you.

We don't settle anymore—not for scraps of love or roles in someone else's story. We don't date from fear of our timeline or out of survival tactics. We date with sacred alignment in mind.

You were worthy from birth, sis.

You are no longer Ms. Hold-It-Down, Ride-or-Die, Fixer, or Savior. You are: "Every woman—it's all in you."

It's been in you all along.

Your inner child can now smile because you are the woman you've always dreamed of being. And due to the work you've done, you now set the tone for your lineage. You've built a legacy of healthy relationships. No more generational trauma passed down in your family. What will be passed down is love, confidence, courage, strength, and the ability to walk away from anything that doesn't serve them—a fighting chance—a foundation that sets them up for greatness.

Now that they don't have to waste 30 years trying to learn and unlearn toxic traits and behaviors from their childhood, they have a much better chance of advancing in life.

I now invite you to live this out—yes sis, IN REAL TIME. You don't have to wait until everything is perfect—start now. Make the call now. Drop that toxic trait, pattern, person, or relationship now. Make the necessary changes in your life so you can succeed and let go of the old things that left you broken, drained, frustrated, and ultimately stole your hope.

If you've made it this far, it has already begun! Remember: healing is not linear. It's layered. It can be messy, hard to navigate, and sometimes difficult to know what to do in the moment. But know this—it's worth it. And you're worth it.

I invite and encourage you to continue doing the work, even beyond these pages. This book is a mirror, but you are the masterpiece. This is nothing to take lightly or minimize. This is sacred work. Honor it. Honor what you are doing. Treat it as you would tell a man to treat you—like a queen.

Worthiness is non-negotiable. That should be the beginning of your new affirmation. Start with that and add the rest to it.

Here are a few more to help you in this process:

- "I deserve love that doesn't ask me to shrink."
- "I am worthy of someone who sees the whole of me and stays."
- "I will never again build a partner from my place of pain."

Understand this: There is a love that uplifts—not unravels. There are relationships where peace is the norm, not the reward for over-functioning. But first, it starts with you. You must believe it— and believe it for YOU. Start investing in this healing by putting things in place.

For instance:

- Seek therapy or coaching.
- Take a sabbatical from dating and recommit to your values.
- Create a circle of safe sisters to support you on this journey.

And so I, Monique R. Darnell, your therapy coach for the recovery of unhealed abandonment wounds, trauma, and inner child restoration—for some, your minister of healing—commission you to go out and date again, love again, and choose from your healed self, not your hidden wounds.

Go date with dignity and abundance.
Go love from overflow.
Go demand softness.
Go be healed out loud, sis.

Know this: Your healing is the most rebellious thing you'll ever do in a world that profits from your pain. But that's okay—because we weren't created to carry them or pay that price.

May you never again build what breaks you.
May your heart choose peace over potential.
May your love be as healed as your hope.

Sis... Look at You Now

A Love Letter for Your Becoming

You didn't just finish a book.
You finished a cycle.
You buried old survival patterns.
You laid down the weight of proving.
You finally said yes to you.
And I'm so proud of you.

I know what it cost to keep turning these pages.
I know how many tears were wiped in silence.
I know the moments when your heart whispered,
"This is me... I've been carrying this."

But now—look at you.
Soft. Still. Sacred.
And no longer begging for what you've already become.

You are no longer trying to build-a-bae-r from your brokenness.
You are becoming the healed woman your younger self prayed for.
You are walking in a peace that doesn't perform.
You are loving from a place that doesn't lack.

You are receiving what aligns
because you no longer chase what abandons.

There is joy here now.
There is clarity.
There is rest.
And maybe, for the first time in a long time—there is you.

Whole.
Worthy.
Here.
Healed.

So go live like it.
Laugh out loud again.
Take yourself out.
Say yes to softness.
Say no to what doesn't honor you.
Let love find you—
because now it will have to meet you at your standard.

I love you.
I celebrate you.
And I am so glad you stayed with yourself
long enough to make it here.

You are not what you've been through.
You are who you chose to become.

Now go be her.
Go be free.

— Monique R. Darnell

Thank you, BAE-R

From Build-A-BAE-R to Becoming Me —
Thank You for Letting Me Go

There's no version of my healing
where your presence isn't part of the beginning.
Not because we made it to forever.
Not because the ending was what I once prayed for or longed for.
But because you were the spark that lit the fire—
a part of me I didn't even know was waiting to be seen.

Before you, I didn't know I could be soft.
Before you, I didn't know I could cry without apologizing for it.
Before you, I didn't know I was carrying my whole childhood
in the way I loved.

You didn't fix me.
But you slowed me down.
You made space for my emotions
when I was still afraid to feel them.

You made me look at myself— not just the strong parts,
but the tender, unfinished ones, too.
You gave me a place to breathe.

A place to unravel.
A place to be seen.

I called you, Boo Bae-r.
And somehow, that name held more truth
than either of us could see at the time.
You were tall, warm, and quiet—
gentle in your presence and silent with your love.
It was the kind of softness that disarmed my armor.

You were comfort in human form,
a resting place I didn't know I was allowed to long for.
But the truth is,
you couldn't hold what you awakened.

You showed me the softness I was capable of—
but were threatened when it required more than you had to give.
And still, I'm grateful.

Because "Boo Bae-r" didn't just describe you—
it taught me that I was never too strong
to need and want tenderness.
That even the strongest woman deserves to be held,
not just by someone else,
but eventually—by herself.

And maybe that's why I stayed longer than I should've.
Maybe that's why I tolerated more than I knew I deserved.
Because for the first time, I wasn't being ghosted.
I wasn't being gaslit.
I was just being… held.

Even when it got messy.
Even when we danced in trauma—
me with my anxious heart,
you with your avoidant silence.

Build-A-BAE-R (Bae Edition)

Even when we left and returned like waves
chasing a shore we both didn't know how to rest on—
I stayed.

I grieved you for a long time.
Two years of circling pain.
Two years of holding hope and heartbreak in the same breath.
Two years of mistaking emotional flashbacks for compatibility.
Two years of realizing that what you gave me…
wasn't what you could sustain.

And still—I thank you.
Not out of bitterness. Not out of fantasy.
But out of reverence.

Because you were the man who helped me meet
the woman underneath my performance.
The woman who thought she had to build love
to be worthy of receiving it.

The woman who thought if she just…
tried harder,
gave more,
fixed more,
he would finally stay…
or it would finally work.

You couldn't stay, nor could I.
Because you weren't ready.
And I wasn't ready to let go of the girl
who begged for love that felt like peace.

But in breaking my heart, you revealed what I had ignored:
The hypervigilant strong Black woman who never felt safe.
The little girl who learned to fix others to feel loved.
The woman who forgot she was enough without building a thing.

So now, I say this with every ounce of compassion and clarity in me:
Thank you.
For the softness.
For the sorrow.
For the space you gave me to see myself.
For not shaming me when I unraveled.
For never calling me "too much."
For holding me without trying to save me.

It didn't work out, and I didn't stay.
But you didn't run from my feelings.
You didn't make me feel like I was too much, nor too emotional.
And that was the beginning of my becoming.

I will always love you for what you were.
But I don't love you more than I love myself anymore.
You were the catalyst, not the keeper.
You were the mirror, not the match.

If you ever come back, you'll meet a new woman.
She doesn't chase.
She doesn't shrink.
She doesn't build bae-rs.
She builds boundaries.
She builds altars.
She builds legacy.

I have moved on—
not because the love wasn't real,
but because my healing is.

And that healing…
it birthed this book.
This journey.
This freedom.
This voice.

This peace.
This version of me.

So thank you, Bae-r.
You weren't the one.
But you were the one who led me back to myself.
And for that… I will always be grateful.

— Monique R. Darnell

Unstuffed, Unbothered, and Unavailable —
Still, Thank You, Bae-r

This is Goodbye!

Appendices: Resources for Further Healing

Sound Healing: What She Needed to Hear All Along

These affirmations were crafted for every stage of your healing—when you're questioning your worth, when you're reclaiming your story, and when you're walking in your wholeness. Speak them. Write them. Believe them. Let them be the soundtrack of your becoming.

You no longer perform to be loved.
You no longer build from brokenness.
You are *built*. You are *healed*. You are *affirmed*.

1. Affirmations for Emotional Healing
For the woman learning to feel deeply and trust her heart again

- I am safe to feel all of my emotions without shame or suppression.
- My pain is valid, but it does not define me.
- I honor every part of my journey—even the broken pieces.

- I release what was never mine to carry.
- My healing is a holy act of resistance and restoration.

2. Affirmations for Reclaiming Identity & Worth

For the woman unlearning lies and embracing her wholeness

- I am already enough—nothing missing, nothing broken.
- I do not have to shrink to be loved.
- I am not a project to be fixed; I am a person to be cherished.
- I release every narrative that told me I was too much or not enough.
- My worth is not negotiable—it is God-ordained.

3. Affirmations for Spiritual Alignment

For the woman reconnecting with God beyond shame, performance, or fear

- God delights in me, even in my becoming.
- I am not being punished—I am being prepared.
- My relationship with God is intimate, personal, and liberating.
- I am held, even when I feel undone.
- I walk in both faith and therapy, and I honor God in my healing.

4. Affirmations for Healthy Love & Relationships

For the woman refusing to build another bae-r from her brokenness

- I deserve a love that feels like peace, not pressure.
- I no longer chase—I choose.
- I only entertain what aligns with my healed heart and sacred standards.
- I do not settle; I select with discernment and dignity.
- I am worthy of a love that honors the whole of me.

5. Affirmations for Legacy & Becoming
For the woman walking boldly into her next chapter

- I am the answered prayer of generations before me.
- I am not starting over—I am starting healed.
- I don't just survive anymore—I thrive on purpose.
- My healing is birthing new possibilities and generational freedom.
- I rise in the fullness of who I am—unapologetic, anointed, and alive.

Soul Questions: The Becoming Beneath the Pages

This book was never just about reading—it was about returning. Returning to your truth. Your power. Your divine rhythm. Each chapter invited you to unlearn, to remember, and to rebuild. But the real transformation begins when you sit with the questions.

These reflections were designed not to fix you—but to FREE you. To help you break patterns, grieve what was, and align with the healed version of yourself who no longer begs, chases, or shrinks.

Take your time. Breathe. Be honest. This is your becoming.

Recognizing Abandonment Wounds & Personal Origins

1. When did you first become aware that something was "missing" emotionally in your relationships?
2. What did love look and feel like in your home growing up?
3. Who did you feel you had to be to receive love?
4. How do you define abandonment—not just physically, but emotionally and spiritually?
5. In what ways did you learn to suppress your emotional needs as a child?
6. How has your family normalized or denied emotional abandonment?

7. When you think about your earliest experiences of love, what emotions come up?
8. What beliefs about love and relationships did you inherit that no longer serve you?
9. How do your abandonment wounds shape your expectations in romantic connections?
10. What patterns do you notice in the kind of "bae-r" you've tried to build in past relationships?

Defining the Root & Recognizing the Signs

1. In what ways were your emotional needs inconsistently met growing up?
2. What moments in your childhood felt like rejection, even if no one used those words?
3. How do you currently respond to perceived or real rejection in relationships?
4. What triggers your fear of being "too much" or "not enough"?
5. Do you see yourself tying your self-worth to how others respond to you?
6. What relationships have you sabotaged because you expected to be left?
7. What role does approval play in your decision-making today?
8. How does your body respond when you feel emotionally unsafe?
9. In what ways does your nervous system still feel "on guard"?
10. What do you need to hear today to begin soothing that inner child?

Patterns, Beliefs, & Emotional Dysregulation

1. How do you behave when you feel someone is pulling away?

2. Do you tend to over-function or over-give in relationships? Why?
3. What kind of people are you typically drawn to, and what do they mirror back to you?
4. What does "safety" mean to you in the context of love?
5. How does your abandonment wound influence your attachment style?
6. Where do you feel like you're always auditioning for love?
7. How do you respond when your needs aren't met—withdrawal, panic, silence, pursuit?
8. What beliefs do you hold about why love hasn't "worked" for you yet?
9. When was the last time you ignored your intuition to avoid being alone?
10. What truth are you finally ready to stop running from?

Understanding Trauma's Influence on Love & Attachment

1. How has your definition of love been shaped by what hurt you?
2. In what ways have you confused intensity or chaos with passion?
3. What unmet childhood needs have you tried to fulfill through romantic relationships?
4. What's one relationship that reflected more of your trauma than your truth?
5. How have you tried to control love as a means of staying safe?
6. When you think about attachment, do you lean toward chasing, avoiding, or over-accommodating?
7. How has codependency shown up in your life (emotionally, spiritually, financially)?
8. What are you most afraid will happen if you stop "fixing" or "rescuing" others?

9. How do you define clarity in relationships—and have you allowed yourself to sit in it?

10. What does choosing love from a healed place look like for you?

Emotional Blueprinting & Pattern Breaking

1. What did your caregivers unintentionally teach you about emotional availability?

2. When did you start believing that love had to be earned or proved?

3. In what ways have you tried to build or "customize" a partner to fit your emotional voids?

4. Who have you loved more for their potential than for their actual presence?

5. What need were you hoping to fulfill by trying to fix or rescue someone else?

6. Are you more comfortable giving love or receiving it? Why?

7. What happens inside you when someone cannot meet your emotional needs?

8. What parts of you were neglected that still crave acknowledgment?

9. What patterns are you now ready to break, even if it means being alone for a season?

10. What would it look like to choose a partner from your wholeness rather than your wounds?

Rejection, Ghosting, and Emotional Release

1. How do you interpret being ghosted or rejected—what story do you tell yourself?

2. What emotions surface when someone disappears without closure?

3. How have you internalized rejection as a reflection of your worth

4. What do you often assume people are thinking about you when they leave or withdraw?

5. What's the difference between being abandoned and being redirected?

6. How do you emotionally self-soothe when someone you care about disappoints you?

7. What part of you is still waiting for an apology or explanation that may never come?

8. What have you clung to that was already emotionally gone?

9. What does releasing attachment to someone who can't love you well feel like in your body?

10. How are you learning to ground yourself in self-worth rather than someone else's response?

Cultural Expectations, Fear of Rejection & Self-Love

1. What did the women in your family teach you—directly or indirectly—about what love requires?

2. Have you ever felt like you had to compete to be chosen or worthy? Where does that come from?

3. How do societal expectations of Black women (strong, selfless, sacrificing) show up in your dating patterns?

4. What did "being a good woman" mean to you growing up—and how has that definition changed?

5. In what ways has fear of rejection led you to shrink or silence yourself?

6. How have you overextended yourself in relationships out of fear of being abandoned again?

7. How does your inner girl still long for affirmation, love, or approval?

8. What does self-love look like when no one is watching?

9. When you think of being "enough," what emotions rise up?

10. How can you begin loving yourself with the same depth you've tried to love others?

Faith, Obedience, Survival & Self-Trust

1. How has your faith tradition shaped your ideas about submission, love, and worthiness?
2. Were you ever taught to "stay" or "pray it away" instead of heal and walk away?
3. How has survival-mode obedience shown up in your romantic or spiritual life?
4. In what ways have you performed for love or acceptance —at church, in relationships, or in family systems?
5. What is the difference between spiritual alignment and emotional suppression in your life?
6. Have you ever confused "obedience" with abandoning your own voice?
7. When did you start questioning the belief that suffering equals spiritual strength?
8. Where in your life have you distrusted your intuition to maintain external peace?
9. What would self-trust look like in your relationships today?
10. What inner truths are you ready to honor without apology?

Healing, Reattachment & Community Restoration

1. What patterns have you repeated in relationships—even when you knew they were harmful?
2. Where did those patterns come from—who modeled them for you?
3. How have you historically responded to loneliness, and what does that say about your wounds?
4. What boundaries have you struggled to set because of fear, guilt, or people-pleasing?
5. What would it look like to reparent your inner child with gentleness and consistency?

6. How do you define "secure love" now versus how you defined it 5 years ago?
7. In what ways have you already begun the work of healing, even if imperfectly?
8. Who are the emotionally safe people in your life—and how can you lean into those connections?
9. What's one area of your life where you still crave outside validation, and how can you bring that back inward?
10. How does healing in community feel different than healing alone?

Self-Love, Inner Child Healing, & Self-Esteem Restoration

1. Who told you who you were—and who do you say you are now?
2. How has abandonment distorted your sense of self-worth?
3. What parts of your identity were shaped by pain rather than truth?
4. What did your inner child need to hear that she never received?
5. How do you tend to your emotional needs without guilt or shame?
6. What are three ways you can begin to reparent yourself today?
7. How have you abandoned yourself in order to be chosen?
8. In what moments do you feel most aligned with your authentic self?
9. What are you no longer willing to negotiate about your value?
10. Who are you becoming now that you no longer settle for survival?

Emotional Safety, Narrative Change & Releasing Limiting Beliefs

1. Where in your life have you struggled to set or maintain boundaries? Why?
2. What story have you been telling yourself about love—and is it still serving you?
3. What beliefs about relationships were rooted in fear or scarcity?
4. How can you honor your own needs without feeling selfish or guilty?
5. What does emotional safety feel like in your body and spirit?
6. Where have you allowed access to people who haven't earned your vulnerability?
7. How would your life change if you believed you are deeply worthy of joy, rest, and peace?
8. What boundaries do you need to set with yourself to stay in alignment with your healing?
9. How will you rewrite your love story starting today?

Integration, Self-Awareness, and the Sacred Call to Wholeness

1. What are three things you've learned about yourself during this healing journey?
2. How has your understanding of love changed since beginning this book?
3. What does healing look like for you now—not as an idea, but as a lifestyle?
4. What emotions do you feel when you say, "I am worthy of healthy love"?
5. What does it mean to choose love from a place of wholeness instead of need?
6. How will you hold yourself accountable to the growth you've experienced?

7. What would it feel like to live as your most healed self every day?
8. What legacy are you now creating with your healing?
9. What does it mean to move forward without apology, without shrinking?
10. How will you honor this version of yourself—the one who chose to heal?

Resources & Support

You don't have to heal alone. Here are tools, voices, and spaces to support your becoming.

Podcasts for Your Healing & Wholeness

1. Therapy for Black Girls
Hosted by Dr. Joy Harden Bradford
Mental health, relationships, and personal growth for Black women
www.therapyforblackgirls.com/podcast

2. Black Girls Heal
Hosted by Shena Lashey
Healing abandonment, reparenting, and learning to love without performing
www.blackgirlsheal.org

3. The Love Hour Podcast
Hosted by Kev & Melissa Fredericks
Archived podcast on healing communication and emotional intimacy

4. Balanced Black Girl
Hosted by Les Alfred
Mindfulness, softness, and wellness tools for Black women.
www.balancedblackgirl.com

Books That Speak to the Soul

- **All About Love** by bell hooks
- **Set Boundaries, Find Peace** by Nedra Glover Tawwab
- **The Body Keeps the Score** by Dr. Bessel van der Kolk
- **Sacred Rest** by Dr. Saundra Dalton-Smith
- **What Happened to You?** by Oprah Winfrey & Dr. Bruce Perry
- **You Are a Badass** by Jen Sincero
- **The Inner Work of Relationships** by Matthew McKay & Patrick Fanning
- **The Garden Within** by Dr. Anita Phillips
- **Woman Evolve, Power Moves, Colliding With Destiny** by Sarah Jakes Roberts

Faith-Based Tools for the Soul, Spirit & Mind

- **Soul Space App** — Christian meditations and Scripture-based reflections: www.soulspace.co

- **Dr. Anita Phillips** — Spirit-led therapist and author blending faith with emotional health: www.dranitaphillips.com

- **Dr. Thema Bryant** — *The Homecoming Podcast* — Wisdom and faith-filled trauma recovery: www.drthema.com

- **Sarah Jakes Roberts** — Preacher, author, and cycle-breaker for women evolving: www.womanevolve.com

- **YouVersion Bible App** — Reading plans and devotionals for emotional and spiritual growth: www.bible.com

- **Morgan Harper Nichols** — Visual poetry, affirmations, and reflections rooted in God's love: www.morganharpernichols.com

Therapy & Support Resources

Books & Self-Awareness Tools

- **You Are a Badass** by Jen Sincero
- **The Inner Work of Relationships** by Matthew McKay & Patrick Fanning

TED Talks & YouTube Education

- *"The Power of Vulnerability"* by Brené Brown
- *"How Childhood Trauma Affects Health Across a Lifetime"* by Nadine Burke Harris
- *"Every Kid Needs a Champion"* by Rita Pierson
- YouTube search terms: *Anxious Attachment, Avoidant Attachment, Healing the Inner Child, Attachment Styles in Love*

Therapist Directories

- **Therapy for Black Girls** — www.therapyfor-blackgirls.com

* * *

Therapy is sacred. Healing is layered. And wholeness is your birthright. Take what you need, return to it as often as you must, and know you are never alone in this work.

Acknowledgments

To my sister and friend, KeyKey— you saw what I couldn't. You saw a message, a mission, and a mirror for the people. You helped me push this book into being, and for that, I will always be grateful. Though our friendship didn't make it to this chapter, your part in this birth will never be erased. I honor you for the role you played in helping me see what needed to be said.

To the "bae-rs" I built— thank you for teaching me what could never truly hold me. You revealed the hollow places in me that I tried to fill with performance, perfection, and proximity. This is not a bitter chapter—this is a burial and a becoming.

To *me*— to the new season, new standard, and new softness I now claim. To the healed eyes I see with, and the restored heart I now protect.

To the little Monique, the little girl who handed out pieces of herself just to feel whole— I love you. You got me here. Every version of you made this version possible.

About the Author

Monique R. Darnell is a multi-state Licensed Professional Counselor, author, speaker, and emotional wellness advocate specializing in culturally attuned mental health care. Her journey into the healing profession began when she stepped into motherhood and encountered the deep, unspoken wounds carried across generations. That awakening led her to pursue her Master's in Mental Health Counseling from Capella University, where she formalized her calling into a lifelong commitment to soul-level restoration.

She is a Certified Advanced Alcohol and Drug Counselor (CAADC), a Certified Clinical Mental Health Counselor (CCMHC) in Georgia, a National Certified Counselor (NCC) through the National Board for Certified Counselors, a Master's Level Certified Addiction Professional (MCAP) in Florida, and a Licensed Mental Health Counselor in Georgia, Florida, and Texas. Her clinical work spans individual and family therapy, addiction recovery, somatic healing, psychoeducation, and holistic life coaching.

Monique's work centers on the emotional and spiritual liberation of Black women and underserved communities. With a deep understanding of religious conditioning, cultural survivalism, and identity trauma, she offers a sacred and affirming approach that bridges faith, therapy, and embodied healing.

As a faith-rooted therapist, Monique is passionate about dismantling emotional barriers caused by generational trauma, religious conditioning, and systemic oppression—especially among Black women who often carry the burden of being strong for everyone but themselves.

Monique's mission is to make mental wellness sacred, accessible, and culturally resonant. Through her writing, counseling, and community engagement, she offers a healing space where faith meets therapy and survival transforms into thriving.

To get in touch with Monique:

mrdcasolutions@gmail.com
https://www.mrdcasolutions.com